T0367230

TIGER, TYRANT, BANDIT, BUSINESSMAN

Brian DeMare

TIGER, TYRANT, BANDIT, BUSINESSMAN

Echoes of Counterrevolution from New China

Stanford University Press
Stanford, California

Stanford University Press
Stanford, California

© 2022 by Brian James DeMare. All rights reserved.

No part of this book may be reproduced or transmitted in any form or by any means, electronic or mechanical, including photocopying and recording, or in any information storage or retrieval system without the prior written permission of Stanford University Press.

Printed in the United States of America on acid-free, archival-quality paper

Library of Congress Cataloging-in-Publication Data
Names: DeMare, Brian James, author.
Title: Tiger, tyrant, bandit, businessman : echoes of counterrevolution
   from New China / Brian DeMare.
Description: Stanford, California : Stanford University Press, 2022. |
   Includes bibliographical references and index.
Identifiers: LCCN 2021051939 (print) | LCCN 2021051940 (ebook) | ISBN
   9781503632363 (cloth) | ISBN 9781503632516 (ebook)
Subjects: LCSH: Counterrevolutionaries—China—Poyang Xian—History. |
   Trials (Political crimes and offenses)—China—Poyang Xian—History. |
   Poyang Xian (China)—History—20th century. | China—History—1949–1976.
Classification: LCC DS797.57.P683 D46 2022 (print) | LCC DS797.57.P683
   (ebook) | DDC 951.05—dc23/eng/20211109
LC record available at https://lccn.loc.gov/2021051939
LC ebook record available at https://lccn.loc.gov/2021051940

Cover design: Kevin Barrett Kane

For Nina. For Miles.

CONTENTS

A FEW WORDS BEFORE WE BEGIN

On a deadly summer night in 1949 Big Tiger led an assassination squad through the mountains of northern Jiangxi, a landlocked province in eastern China. For the crimes he and his saber committed that evening, he became one of the first to be charged by the Chinese Communist Party as an *evil tyrant*. This was a criminal label that the party gave to villagers accused of abusing and exploiting their neighbors. A conviction would make Big Tiger a *counterrevolutionary*, worthy of execution for attempting to forestall the liberation of the masses. Many would follow his long and winding path through the justice system of the People's Republic of China, but the voices of the rural folk accused of counterrevolution are largely absent from the historical record. That's no longer the case for Big Tiger, whose tale of crime and punishment is detailed in this book's second casefile.

There are other uncommon voices in this book. Readers will hear from Golden Cao, a bandit who came down from a mountainous hideout to spill his guts to the Communists. And from Merchant Zha, a hapless businessman, tried for spying on the behalf of a feared counterrevolutionary army. To these voices this book adds those of farmers, administrators, secret society members, and a Confucian gentleman with a bum left foot. It seems prudent to admit from the start that these voices didn't come to me unfiltered. They arrived as textual echoes, bouncing through four criminal casefiles, each filled with reports and confessions filed away by bureaucrats working at the lowest levels of the Chinese state.

For over 2,000 years the county represented the furthest reaches of government administration in China. Well into the twentieth century, the formal power of the state went no further than county-level bureaucrats. The documents generated by these local governments offer some of the closest access to rural China at what historians call the *grassroots*: the lower reaches of society, populated by the ordinary folk who endured decades of revolutionary upheavals and state building programs. This book is based on a particularly unique set of documents: four criminal casefiles, all produced by county-level security officers in the first years of the People's Republic. Each casefile concerns an investigation into counterrevolution in Poyang, an overwhelmingly rural county in northern Jiangxi. This book, however, is not just about counterrevolution. The rare voices found in this book reveal much about the countryside and what the revolution meant for all rural citizens. Because the documents used to create this book offer an unflinching perspective on China's recent past, readers should be warned that the following pages contain graphic descriptions of violence, often directly narrated by the accused.

I spent some time in the countryside around Poyang County in the summer of 2004. By the time I got to northern Jiangxi, the revolutionary furor of those early days seemed a long-forgotten memory. Blissfully unaware of the criminal cases profiled in this book and visiting a particularly idyllic corner of rural China at a formative time in my life, I was deeply impressed by the rustic beauty of the countryside and the fine hospitality of Jiangxi villagers. Even now, many years later, I still remember much of that trip. I hitched rides on the backs of motorcycles with broken speedometers as I zipped from village to village. I shared a pot of tea with an elderly woman, who invited me into her house and regaled me with stories of the Cultural Revolution. She was eager to brag about her son, then teaching ping-pong in Germany.

When I first began working with these four criminal cases, I didn't make the connection between the files and my own experiences in the northern Jiangxi countryside. All I knew was that these types of documents were exceedingly rare, and I was hopeful that they might contain a revealing anecdote or perhaps some data for a scholarly article that my colleagues might find useful. As I worked my way through the casefiles over the past few years, the documents exceeded all expectations. Individually, each casefile contains a tremendous tale, complete with relatable characters, plot twists, and no shortage of drama. And each is unique in both its nature and what it reveals about those years as the Communists set up shop in the countryside. Most tantalizing, the four casefiles offered the chance to hear, however indirectly, from the rural folk who personally experienced this most pivotal moment of rural revolution.

Composed of a bewildering mix of documents, the casefiles didn't give up their secrets easily, if at all. Read from front to back, they don't make much sense. Even individual documents within the casefiles reject chronological narratives, jumping back and forth between events and characters with no regard for readers. Many of the documents are summary reports filed by security officers, but other texts offer transcriptions of interrogations and confessions. Some were penned directly by rural citizens, including defiant statements of innocence from the accused. Overall, I'm thankful that the bureaucratic nature of the People's Republic, said to result in "mountains of meetings and seas of documents," created such dense casefiles.

I quickly realized that while the casefiles were overflowing with detail, figuring out what exactly happened would be a true challenge. This book's narrative structure is the result of my attempt to make sense of the four criminal investigations and the echoes I found in the documents. But there is no single narrative in any of the casefiles, let alone a single voice. Some confessions are signed by multiple witnesses, further confusing any understanding of authorship. The documents are full of contradictions and errors, creating much confusion and angst as I worked my way through this project. In recent years I have found myself increasingly drawn to stories told by unreliable narrators, so perhaps it's fitting that while reinvestigating these casefiles I had little choice but to continually question my sources at every turn. Were security officers willfully misrepresenting the crimes of men they assumed to be evil counterrevolutionaries? Might village cadres put their careers before the truth? Were rural accusers speaking honestly about past injustices, or were they fabricating crimes in search of personal gain? Knowing the long history of innocents falsely admitting guilt to avoid harsher punishments, could I trust any confession?

The documents themselves, meanwhile, presented unique challenges, starting with unidentifiable authors, dates, and titles. Authors sometimes used scraps of paper, or stationery recycled from the previous Nationalist regime. Many words were faded beyond recognition. Semi-literate authors often used incorrect characters. The transition from lunar to solar calendars, one of the many changes in what the Communists called New China, complicated my attempts to provide exact dates for murders, jail-breaks, and trials. All too often, the echoes of the past faded beyond recognition. In a particularly grievous textual crisis, I realized that I couldn't say with certainty if a victim discussed in one of the cases was an armed soldier or an innocent bystander, caught in the wrong place at the wrong time.

Many hours passed as I sought connections between the archival documents and published accounts of the county, to say nothing of the larger history of rural China as the Communists came to power. I dare not calculate how long I spent staring at digital maps, desperately hoping that satellite imagery might shed some perspective on murders long forgotten. I still curse, from the bottom of my historian heart, the engineers who coldly flooded Hengyong Township under a gigantic reservoir. I endeavored to make these criminal investigations legible, even to readers unfamiliar with the history of modern China. It was my hope that these four cases might provide readers with a sense of this moment in time and inspire them to read more about the decades that followed. Perhaps a few of them would search for documents themselves, to see what voices and tales they might contain.

I designed this book as an investigation into four criminal cases, but along the way I realized I would have to say something about the history of the towns and villages where these crimes and trials took place. The book begins with "The Setting," a brief introduction to Poyang County, with a focus on the problem of ruling rural China, and how the rivalry between the Communist and Nationalist parties shaped local politics. "The Setting" is followed by four investigations, one for each of the four casefiles. Casefile 1 details the deadly alliance between bandits and secret society men that assaulted a Communist outpost. In casefile 2 readers will hear from Big Tiger as he is brought to justice for his role in a brutal midnight assassination. Casefile 3 puts the spotlight on a runaway landlord who went undercover as a secret agent to save his own life. And in casefile 4, a failed businessman takes a Kafkaesque journey through the rapidly evolving legal system of the People's Republic. At the close of each investigation, I pause to highlight some of the issues raised by each case, as well as some of the archival problems that vexed me as a historian. And because this book is a small contribution to a vibrant academic field, I'll suggest further readings to help point the way to some incredible scholarship.

Readers may have noted that I used the term "New China" in the title of this book. This was no accident. The Communists loudly boasted that their liberation of the countryside cast off the legacies of imperial and Nationalist rule and created a New China. As a historian I urge my students to consider the many connections between the People's Republic and earlier regimes. And yet, reading these four casefiles, it's hard to ignore how much was new in these early years as the Communists brought state power into villages and down to the grassroots. The Communist regime inherited Poyang in all its dysfunctional glory. In the decades before the dawn of New China, the county government had almost no authority in the countryside. The arrival of the Communists heralded decisive changes. What would happen to the mountain outlaws? Lineage organizations that placed family before the state? Religious practices that gave comfort to rural citizens? Merchants trying to eke out a profit in the midst of political and social upheavals? The tales that follow are a direct outgrowth of the conflict between Communist statecraft and the long-standing traditions of the Chinese countryside.

TIMELINE OF EVENTS

1949

February
Casefile 4: General Li returns home to Poyang.

April
People's Liberation Army arrives in Poyang.

May 1
Cadres celebrate the liberation of Poyang Town.

June 15
Casefile 1: Golden Cao and the Eastern Mountain Ridge bandits attack
   Xiejiatan.

July 4
Casefile 1: Boss Wang leads an attack on a work team in Hengyong
   Township.
Casefile 2: Landlords plot the murder of Comrade Zhou in Dayuan Village.

July 5
Casefile 1: Old Six leads an ambush on Pig Mouth Mountain.

July 6
Casefile 1: Old Seven leads an assault on Chuanwan.
Casefile 2: Landlords meet with Big Tiger to plan the assassination of
   Comrade Zhou.

July 8
Casefile 2: Big Tiger leads an assassination squad in Dayuan Village.

July 13
Casefile 4: Secretary Zhou martyred in Xiejiatan.

July
Provincial leaders issue a directive on "weeding out traitors."

October 1
People's Republic of China founded in Beijing.

1950

January 10
Jiangxi leaders call for work units to conduct an "internal cleansing."

February
Casefile 4: Merchant Zha resigns from the People's Government.

March
Poyang County People's Tribunal established.

April
Campaigns against evil tyrants begin in Poyang.
Casefile 4: Merchant Zha opens his oil press.

May 8
Casefile 2: Filial Zhou charges Big Tiger with murder.

June
Land reform campaigns begin in Poyang.

July
Casefile 1: Final confession from Scholarly Wu, Golden Cao, and
    General Hong.

October

Casefile 4: Hengxi Township cadres confront Merchant Zha over the oil
    press.

November

"Directive Concerning the Suppression of Counterrevolutionary
    Activities" issued.

November 15

Casefile 4: Merchant Zha arrested.

November 19

Casefile 3: Landlord Hua arrested.

December 11

Casefile 2: Big Tiger arrested.

1951

January

Casefile 4: Merchant Zha declared guilty by a branch of the People's
    Tribunal.

February 22

Casefile 3: Three criminal landlords break out of jail.

March 23

Casefile 2: Judge Jiang, Poyang county-chief, sentences Big Tiger to
    death.

June 25

Casefile 4: Judge Wang reduces Merchant Zha's sentence.

July 9

Casefile 3: Runaway Xu turns himself in to the county Public Security
    Bureau.

August 9
Casefile 3: Security officers arrest the ringleaders of the Bodhisattva
   Society.

1952

April 28
Casefile 2: Big Tiger executed.

June 20
Casefile 4: Merchant Zha walks free.

TIGER, TYRANT, BANDIT, BUSINESSMAN

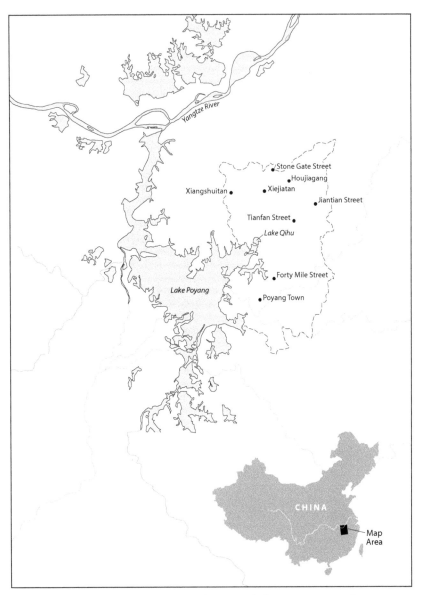

Map 1. Poyang County, its surroundings, and the approximate locations of some of the central events in the numbered casefiles. Lake Poyang connects to the Yangtze River, which flows west to east.

THE SETTING

The County by the Lake

This book dives deep into four criminal cases, all of which occurred in a modest corner of rural China many decades ago. These explorations of bandit uprisings, midnight assassinations, fugitives on the run, and counterrevolutionaries on trial emphasize the perspectives of the villagers and townsfolk who found themselves entangled in the legal system. All four of these cases, however, were originally investigated by security officers working for the newly established People's Republic of China as they attempted to tame the countryside for the Chinese Communist Party. Nearly everything we know about these cases comes to us through documents left by these officers, who are just as central to the stories told in this book as the accused criminals and their victims.

Few outsiders are familiar with the sliver of Jiangxi Province that serves as the setting for this book, so it may be useful to introduce the county and its history. To complicate matters, the place has gone by a few different names over the years. In ancient times it was simply known as Po. Some old-timers remember when they called it Raozhou. For a few decades, for reasons locals still debate, it was known as Boyang County. But for most of its recent history, it has been named after the massive lake lying directly to its southwest. You can't miss it.

Lake Poyang is China's largest freshwater lake, its vast waters stretching beyond the horizon. To the north the lake reaches into the mighty Yangtze River, which runs from the Tibetan highlands down through China's economic heartland, including the otherwise landlocked province of Jiangxi. Sadly, in recent years the lake has fallen on hard times. When torrential storms arrive in the late summer, Lake Poyang's waters are seemingly everywhere. Coastal communities know the fury of the lake's floods all too well. And during dry months, when the rains stop and the sun continues to beat down on its waters, the lake is reduced to a truly pitiful state. Ever since the completion of the Three Gorges Dam in 2006, Lake Poyang, expansive but never particularly deep, suffers through severe dry spells. For surrounding villages that once relied on the lake for a nearly limitless supply of fresh water and resources, this process of destruction has been a decades-long tale of woe.[1] One recent visitor found fishing boats "laid out in uneven rows, flipped upside down on the moist soil. Around them grasses were growing and cows grazing. It was once all water."[2]

For most of the year, the freshwater sea of Lake Poyang is still a sight to behold. It's not the scenery, however, that has long attracted outsiders to its shores. The strategic importance of Lake Poyang made its coastal communities worthy of attention. The lake, by far the most prominent feature of the region, is vital to local economic life. But Poyang, the largest county by population in Jiangxi and the setting for this book, is far more than its famous lake. For readers interested in the lay of the land, the county is situated in the northeast of Jiangxi Province. Past the county's mountainous north one finds the flowing Yangtze, which serves as the border between northern Jiangxi and neighboring Anhui Province. To the east lies Jingdezhen, a major urban center, famous for the arsenal of kilns that fired out imperial China's finest porcelains. And southwest across the expansive lake lies Nanchang, the provincial capital. As one local saying tells it: "Mountains encircle the northeast, waters converge to the southwest."[3]

In the Footsteps of the Lord of Po

With almost 200 rivers large and small, and over 200 lakes besides Lake Poyang, water is of utmost importance to the county. These waterways and their strategic value brought state power to Poyang. From the very start of the imperial era, Poyang hosted a county government.[4] The county proved the most durable of administrative units. For thousands of years it represented the lowest level in the state's administrative structure, where the immense power of the ruler met the vast reality of the empire.

When the county by the lake was initially created it needed a *magistrate*, an official to serve the emperor and wield state power. Poyang's first magistrate served for ten years, earning a stellar reputation as a model ruler. Later hailed as "Lord of Po" and worshiped at a temple built in his honor, he was revered as a just and diligent magistrate.[5] He established his regime between Mount Zhi and the Rao River, creating what would eventually grow into today's Poyang Town. In one of his most important acts, the Lord of Po mobilized locals to build a city wall, over two miles of fortification that symbolized imperial power from the shores of the lake. The first of many Poyang bureaucrats, he set an impossibly high standard for his successors.

The hundreds of magistrates who followed the Lord of Po during the subsequent centuries, all outsiders and all men, came to Poyang Town on behalf of their emperors to oversee everything from bandit suppression to tax collection. They handled legal affairs and enforced imperial law, serving as both prosecutor and judge. Fan Zhengci, for example, served in Poyang over a thousand years after the Lord of Po oversaw the construction of the town's walls. Judge Fan, a native of Shandong to the far north, is now legendary for investigating and solving criminal cases.[6] But in this regard he wasn't so unique. The bureaucrats in charge of Poyang County passed judgments on accused criminals for centuries as dynasties rose and fell, setting direct precedents for the four criminal cases discussed in this book.

Magistrates served as the only official government representative at county government offices, known as the *yamen*. Their jobs were exceedingly difficult and only got harder over the centuries as population growth undermined their efforts to control their many subjects. At the end of the imperial era, a Poyang magistrate was responsible for the fates of over 800,000 subjects.[7] The only way a magistrate could possibly govern a county as populous as Poyang was by hiring *clerks* and *runners*. These men were the yamen's feared "talons and teeth," doing the dirty work that kept the county government running. Clerks managed the paperwork produced by the yamen, everything from compiling tax rolls to recording criminal confessions. Runners, meanwhile, brought the power of the state out of Poyang Town and into the countryside, venturing into villages to investigate crimes, arrest criminals, and collect taxes.[8] Otherwise, the imperial state largely left villagers to their own devices. Reformers had long dreamed of establishing government offices below the county level. No emperor, however, ever effectively dispatched his bureaucrats past the county yamen. Late imperial states did create administrative units that grouped together subjects to assist taxation and control, but these were run by locals, not loyal bureaucrats.

Rebels and Revolutionaries in Poyang Town

By the dawn of the twentieth century, foreign and domestic strife had pushed the Qing, the final dynasty of the imperial era, to the brink. For decades Qing subjects, seeing ever more evidence of China's weaknesses, vacillated between blaming foreign imperialists and the dynasty's Manchu rulers, who had once been considered non-Chinese barbarians. The fall of the ancient imperial system started with attacks on Westerners and their religion: in 1900 popular anger against Christian missionaries, skillfully channeled by local elites, exploded during the Boxer Uprising. Farmers in North China, trained in simple martial arts and believing themselves invulnerable to bullets, burned churches, killed missionaries and their converts, and flocked to Beijing in support of the Qing. In Nanchang furious protestors destroyed a Christian church and murdered a priest. When word spread across the lake to Poyang Town, locals marched to the church on Desheng Road and burned it down to the ground.[9]

Attacks on Westerners and Christians only increased the threat of imperialist invasion, creating ever more frustration among would-be reformers. In Poyang, as was often the case throughout the empire, ambitious young men such as Jiang Bozhang turned to revolution. Jiang was almost certainly the first Poyang man to join the Revolutionary Alliance, an underground network headed by the charismatic and cosmopolitan Sun Yat-sen. Sun, educated in Hong Kong and Hawaii, was a *nationalist*: he longed for a strong Chinese state, run by and for the Chinese people, and advocated for a revolution that would turn Chinese subjects into Chinese citizens.[10]

In 1911, not long after Jiang Bozhang embraced Sun Yat-sen's revolutionary proposals, uprisings broke out across the empire as Chinese elites removed the Manchus from power. A collection of militarists, determined to make China strong, formed a new government up in Beijing: the Republic of China. Optimism ran high during those first days of the Republic. Sun Yat-sen, widely regarded as a radical rabble-rouser, pledged that his National People's Party, much more commonly called the Nationalists, would work with the new government. The broad alliance that gave many Chinese hope extended down to Poyang, where Nationalist Party member Jiang Bozhang served the new regime as a police-chief.

This alliance proved short lived. Less than a year later, Beijing militarists outlawed the Nationalist Party. Jiang Bozhang fled to Japan, where he had the good fortune to meet up with Sun Yat-sen. The revolution kept moving during his absence from home. In 1921 Soviet agents, dispatched from Moscow, helped establish the Chinese Communist Party in Shanghai; three years later they helped broker an alliance between the Communists and Sun's Nationalists. In many ways they made natural allies. Both sides believed that political mobilization could unite the Chinese people and defeat imperialism. The two parties would soon also share the exact same organizational structure, designed to command compliance from top to bottom. But because the Communists made a point to prioritize the interests of peasants and workers, the alliance was always an uneasy one. The bonds and rivalries between the Nationalists and the Communists would define Chinese politics for the next three decades. Locally, their bitter and deadly battles would set the stage for each of the four cases investigated in this book.

The Revolution Comes to Town

For the moment neither revolutionary party was welcome in Poyang, keeping Jiang Bozhang away from home. During his long absence, the Nationalist Party, and nationalism broadly, continued to grow. Jiang returned to Jiangxi to develop underground Nationalist Party organizations in 1924. Recruiting students at Poyang Academy and other local schools, he established the county branch of the Nationalist Party. Jiang's career in Jiangxi was taking off, and he would spend the next twenty-five years bouncing between Poyang and Nanchang.[11] But he wasn't the only Poyang native advocating for revolution. Young, passionate, and driven by anti-imperialism, Li Xinhan was a prime candidate to join a revolutionary party. But he didn't follow in the footsteps of Jiang Bozhang, who was his senior by eighteen years. Nationalism wasn't enough. For Li it was essential to fight not only imperialists, but class enemies as well. In 1926 Li formally joined the Communist Party and was a founding member of its Poyang party branch. Just like Jiang Bozhang had done a couple of years earlier for the Nationalists, Li did his organizing in secret.[12]

Even as the Communists and the Nationalists remained hidden in Poyang, their alliance, heralded as a grand United Front, allowed both parties to thrive. As the ranks of both parties grew with new recruits, the Nationalists invested heavily in military education and equipment, creating a highly disciplined and politically trained army, the likes of which was previously unheard of in China. The United Front survived the untimely passing of Sun Yat-sen in 1925. The following year Sun's successor Chiang Kai-shek launched the Northern Expedition, a military campaign that aimed to reunify the vast territories then held by dozens of regional warlords. The effort proved a wild success.

With the arrival of Northern Expedition forces in November of 1926, the revolution came to Poyang for the first of many visits. The counties surrounding the lake welcomed the Nationalists. Few farmers had much love for regional warlords.[13] But wealthy elites, fearing what the Nationalists and their revolution might mean for them, fled. Lin Quanfan, the county magistrate, hearing the news of the Northern Expedition's impending arrival, hit the road as well. Magistrate Lin, appointed to Poyang by local militarists, was the last would-be Lord of Po to call himself a magistrate. One of the officers attached to the Northern Expedition took charge of the county government, but he used a much more modern sounding title, which is still in use today: *county-chief*.[14]

The new county regime in Poyang, led by a Northern Expedition veteran, was uniquely inclusive. Working as allies under the United Front, the Nationalists put the county Security Regiment under the command of Li Xinhan, a Communist. Behind the façade of unity, however, the United Front was buckling from within. Under Sun Yat-sen, the Nationalists had attempted to represent all Chinese citizens, but as the revolution deepened during the United Front, Sun's former party struggled to balance the interests of radicals and conservatives. The new head of the Nationalist Party, moreover, was Chiang Kai-shek, a military man and a fervent anti-Com-

munist. As Chiang's power continued to grow with a string of victories
during the Northern Expedition, he turned on his Communist allies in a
bloody purge that left thousands dead: the Shanghai Massacre of April
12, 1927. In Poyang local Nationalists expelled their now-former Communist allies from the county government. Li Xinhan wisely left town,
but not before making off with the weapons of the county Security Regiment, burying thirteen guns and smuggling another ten out of Poyang
Town in a coffin as he disappeared into the countryside.[15]

Land Wars in Poyang

Li Xinhan's quiet sojourn reflected a much larger trend. Since their party's
founding, the Communists had focused nearly all their efforts on promoting urban revolution; now, their work in cities devastated by the Shanghai
Massacre, party organizers increasingly experimented with rural revolution.[16] Li Xinhan took his smuggled Nationalist guns to the Pearl Lake
countryside, where he quickly got to work organizing farmers and training a makeshift militia, directly challenging local powerholders. It was
only a matter of weeks before the Nationalists dispatched the county Security Regiment, recently led by Li himself, to attack the base area. Li's
new men were able to drive off the Security Regiment, but the county
forces injured multiple farmers and arrested another three. Undeterred,
the next day Li rallied over 3,000 Pearl Lake villagers and marched on
Poyang Town. County-chief Song Dexin had no choice but to release the
Pearl Lake prisoners and pay off the injured parties.[17]

Li Xinhan hosted a massive rally in celebration, unaware that the revolution was about to take yet another turn. Back in Poyang Town, his
comrades in the county party branch had been doing their best to lay
low, moving their secret headquarters to avoid detection. But on November 18, 1927, shortly after moving into their new offices near the temple
where locals still worshipped the Lord of Po, they were discovered and
arrested. Just as had been the case back when magistrates interrogated
prisoners at the imperial yamen, county-chief Song sat in judgment of the
three Communists, two men and a woman. Fooled by the young woman's pleas that she was an innocent bystander, county-chief Song set her
free. As for the other two, he had them tortured, paraded through the
streets of Poyang Town, and executed.[18] Within weeks the Nationalists

dispatched an expeditionary force and decimated the Communists' Pearl Lake base area. But Li Xinhan refused to go quietly. He joined up with a band of Communist guerrillas, over 200 strong. They came down from their mountain strongholds to raid targets in Poyang and nearby counties.

While the Communists experimented with rural revolution, Jiang Bozhang's career had been on the rise. In 1930 the Nationalist Party sent him home to serve as county-chief and do something, finally, about those Communists in the countryside.[19] County-chief Jiang went all-out against rural revolutionaries, even dispatching propaganda teams to Poyang villages to spread anti-Communist messages. His most important moves fell under the broad category of "bandit suppression": sending armed forces into the countryside to eradicate any form of resistance. In April 1930 Jiang organized a military force comprised of soldiers drawn from the counties threatened by the Communist guerrillas. Launching an "encircle and annihilate" expedition, his three-pronged attack smashed the guerrilla band's stronghold.[20]

Li Xinhan fled Poyang, only to return with the powerful Red Tenth Army. The Communists finally had a military of note in Poyang, and from August until November the Red Tenth Army roamed throughout the county, reestablishing party organizations and local governments. Most brazenly, the Communists seized Poyang Town and organized attacks on wealthy town residents, emptied the county jail, and redistributed captured wealth. On October 6, 1930, the Communists held a public celebration at the town's main stage, then named in honor of Sun Yat-sen. The over 600 town residents in attendance heard Li Xinhan proclaim the establishment of a new county government, this one run by the Communists. The success of the Red Tenth Army, however, was decidedly fleeting. Shortly after getting run out of Poyang Town, the Red Tenth Army fled from the county by the lake. Jiang Bozhang, still county-chief, dispatched his forces throughout the countryside to destroy any traces of their work, creating no shortage of martyrs. The revolutionary organizations that Li Xinhan and his comrades had seemingly willed into existence collapsed, crushed by the county government Li had once served.[21]

Factionalism and Dysfunction: The 1930s and 1940s

Jiang Bozhang, personally directing the downfall of the Communists, cemented his authority in his home county. He and his fellow Poyang folk ran things in the county in the 1930s and '40s, but local Nationalists split into three rival factions, a reflection of the infighting that made the Republic's national government famously ineffective.[22] Outsiders attempting to run the county had to carefully balance competing interests. Failure to do so could be dangerous. In 1932, for reasons that are still unclear, someone tried to assassinate the newly appointed county-chief.

During these years of factional infighting, the county government grew increasingly unable to carry out its duties. The Nationalists, in an attempt to tighten their control over the countryside, did break with tradition and finally established government offices below the county level. In Poyang the countryside was divided into a handful of districts. These districts, far too large to effectively control the countryside, were occasionally reshuffled and eventually abolished. Below the district government offices, the county government created township, hamlet, and neighborhood administrative units. Township government posts were given out to loyal subordinates. Hamlets and neighborhoods, formed primarily to aid taxation and conscription, were overseen by unpaid locals. Little work got done.[23]

And then, in 1937, locals spotted Japanese fighter planes flying over Lake Poyang. Another war was on its way. The following year, the Nationalists destroyed local railways and mined the lake to slow the Japanese offensive. This was followed by a summer of fierce fighting, with heavy casualties on both sides. The lake, observers said, ran red with the blood of both Japanese and Chinese soldiers.[24] The Japanese, however, were far more interested in Lake Poyang than its surrounding communities. Even Poyang Town was largely left to its own devices during these years. That just meant that factionalism and dysfunction continued to get worse. A falling-out with either faction was dangerous. In 1932 one county-chief had been nearly assassinated. In 1944 Ding Guobing, then in his second year of running the county government, was knifed to death in Poyang Town.[25]

A year later the war against Japan finally ended, but soon bad tidings came again, this time from the north, announcing the start of the latest chapter in the seemingly never-ending conflict between the Communists and the Nationalists. In the aftermath of Japan's surrender, Chiang Kai-shek had been eager to finish off his longtime rivals, woefully miscalculating how much had changed since he had the Communists on the ropes back in the early 1930s. Now led by Mao Zedong, the Communists had found a winning strategy in the countryside, rallying farmers to their cause with promises of land and dignity. The Communists, always attentive to language, made sure to emphasize that their arrival brought about the redemption and renewal of local society, a transformation that they called *liberation*.

The Nationalists, their armies faltering on the battlefield, had never effectively governed the countryside. The departure of Japanese imperialists created a power vacuum in Poyang, but instead of the state it was outlaws and secret societies that rushed in to fill the void. On battlefields far away from Poyang, the Communists decisively crushed their Nationalist rivals and headed south. Jiang Bozhang escaped to Taiwan, the new home for the Republic of China. He had no desire to answer to the Communists for his actions during their last visit. He never set foot in Poyang again.

New China Dawns

Nearly two decades after being chased out of Poyang, the Red Army, now known as the People's Liberation Army, crossed south across the Yangtze River in April 1949. Marching behind these soldiers was a smaller force, this one composed largely of *cadres*, a catch-all term for the political workers who implemented revolution on behalf of the Communists. It was their job to take hold of the county once and for all. Before a single soldier set foot in Poyang, these cadres had already formed party committees and plans for a new county regime: the People's Government. Like the vast majority of bureaucrats before them, they were outsiders. Mostly from the northern provinces of Hebei, Shandong, and Henan, these cadres were unfamiliar with local terrain, customs, and cuisine. Far more troubling, they would have major problems understanding the Gan dialect spoken by Poyang folk.[26]

On April 27 these soldiers and cadres arrived at Stone Gate Street, an important market town in the mountainous north. The road down to Poyang Town opened before them. For the leaders of the old regime, the writing was on the wall. Wu Ji, the last Nationalist to ever serve as county-chief, fled the next day, carrying off the county government's official seal. The town he left behind had seen better days. Its roads and alleyways, over a hundred in all, had long fallen into disrepair. Bumpy and uneven, they were a terror to navigate. Only three of the roads stretched wider than three meters. Some alleyways were less than a meter wide. The town's stout wall, first built during the reign of the Lord of Po, was long gone by the time the Communists showed up. But the town was still the closest thing to an urban center in the county. Residents looked down at visiting villagers, easily identified through subtle but telling divergences in the way they spoke. And Poyang Town certainly boasted the finest marketplace in the county, offering a rich array of wares. Eight bookstores sold everything from Western books to romance novels. At night kerosene lamps illuminated the way, a marked improvement over the oil lamps that lit the late imperial era.[27]

Two days after taking Stone Gate Street, a regiment of soldiers from the Second Field Army, mostly farm boys from the north, reached Poyang Town. All that was left of the Nationalist regime was the county Security Regiment. Back in the 1930s this force had hunted down Communist organizers throughout the countryside. Now they turned the town over to its new Communist rulers. Not a single shot was fired. The new People's Government offered the men the opportunity to stay on and serve the regime. In a clear sign of the fluid loyalties in Poyang, over seventy of them signed up to help the Communists keep order.[28]

The Communists, of course, had been to this town before. They first arrived as part of Chiang Kai-shek's Northern Expedition in 1927, only to be driven into the countryside after the collapse of the United Front. And the Red Tenth Army seized the town in 1930 before Jiang Bozhang and the Nationalists quickly sent them packing. But when the Communists came to town in 1949, they came to stay. The cadres assigned to run the county government, eager to exert their control, quickly took over one of the mainstays of the old regime: the Public Security Bureau. Established back in 1926 when the Nationalists modernized the county government, the bureau was staffed with patrolmen, police officers, and street sweepers, all under a police-chief.[29]

The county's Public Security Bureau, headquartered in Poyang Town, now enforced party justice in Poyang. Back up north, at least a few security officers were abusing the power given to them by the new People's

Republic. According to one local study, officers in a North China county rode their motorcycles to the houses of suspects at night. Breaking down doors, they beat and tormented their victims in the search for evidence.[30] There is no evidence that Poyang officers abused locals in such a manner, but the northern cadres running the Public Security Bureau held real authority. They oversaw an expansive security apparatus, controlling everything from investigating political crimes to running detention centers.[31] Critically, these officers would be on the front lines as the Communists broke with tradition and brought state power out of government offices and into Poyang villages.

At three in the afternoon on May 1, the party celebrated the official liberation of Poyang. The town quickly took on the trappings of what the Communists called *New China*. Some of the first changes were in the names of local streets. The lane that housed imperial and Nationalist government offices was reborn as Liberation Street. Liberation Street ran north to south, perpendicular with May 1st Avenue, named in honor of the day the county was formally declared part of New China. Nanchang, the provincial capital, welcomed the People's Liberation Army three weeks later. Before another month had passed, life began to return to some semblance of normalcy, with commercial boats once again sailing the waters of Lake Poyang.[32] But the transformation of the countryside was just getting started. Imperial governments had been content to rule from Poyang Town. The Nationalists had set up a loose network of local administration, largely leaving villagers to their own devices. The Communists, in stark contrast, were determined to remake rural China from the bottom up.

Down to the Grassroots: Into Village Poyang

Despite the many battles that took place on its freshwater sea, the county by the lake largely avoided the destruction of the Japanese invasion and the subsequent Civil War. This was an overwhelmingly rural place, with little to attract outsiders besides the strategic lake. There wasn't much in the way of modern industry in the county, with sleepy Poyang Town the closest thing to an urban center. Out in the countryside, farming followed ancient practices. As one local explained, villagers

still use buffaloes to pull the plough as the Chinese have been doing for thousands of years; they still use shoulder poles and wheelbarrows to transport goods; they still plant rice by hand, one bunch at a time; and they still thresh rice by hitting the crop against a wooden board. In this respect, nothing has changed.[33]

Poyang farmers grew a diverse portfolio of crops, including beans, watermelons, tobacco, and tea. More than anything else, rice, cultivated in flooded paddy fields, dominated the countryside. Farmers used organic fertilizers of animal and human manure. Without the benefit of insecticides, they relied on birds and frogs to help keep pests under control. Villages were largely self-sufficient and isolated from each other, and seemingly worlds away from the political dramas of Poyang Town. During the winter, village women spun fluffed cotton into yarn using traditional spinning wheels. Women also made shoes and wove wheat and barley straw into hats during the summer months. Bamboo leaves, skillfully crafted into hats, kept villagers dry from the rain. Even bed mattresses, mosquito nets, and quilts were produced in the village. There was almost no commercial interaction between villages, and little social or cultural interchange either. Villages were typically composed of families from a handful of lineages, with many villages named after their most powerful clans. Gravel roads in the countryside were still decades away.[34]

The lake's low and flat alluvial plain covered the southwestern portion of the county where Poyang's many rivers converged. Here, aside from a few wealthy households with sturdy brick houses, most villagers used earthen materials to construct simple shelters. Moving to the northwest travelers encountered hills and eventually high mountain ranges, stretching in unbroken chains, encircling the county. Accounting for nearly one-half of the county's land, these hills and mountains housed bamboo groves and dense forests of conifers and broad-leaved trees. The mountains and their forests were essential to the local economy, providing lumber for housing and for the market. Chinese fir trunks were especially valued for coffins, a major expense in local society and a convenient container for smuggling guns out of Poyang Town. Villagers found endless uses for bamboo, crafting farming and fishing tools and harvesting tender and tasty shoots in the spring and winter.[35]

For decades Poyang villagers had largely escaped the horrors of war, even as Lake Poyang ran red with blood. In 1949, as their long isolation finally ended, many villagers waited with cautious optimism, while many others waited in fear. The arrival of the Communists, however, was slowed considerably by fierce resistance from locals. Some were petty hooligans of little significance, while others grouped together in well-or-ganized armies led by men with clear ties to the Nationalists. The People's Government considered all of them *bandits*, using the very same language that the Nationalists had used when they hunted down Communists in the countryside. The new Jiangxi regime, surveying the province's moun-tains, lakes, and rivers, counted over 37,600 bandits, grouped in some 240 gangs of various sizes. Bringing them to justice presented a true chal-lenge. As some Jiangxi outlaws were known to say: "The People's Libera-tion Army has their soldiers and horses. We have our mountains."[36]

Some of the fiercest resistance, aimed at the heart of the new regime, occurred during the trying summer of 1949. Matters were greatly com-plicated by the widespread collapse of water-control systems, which un-leashed massive floods. During the flooding of that first summer of New China, with water rising five feet high in Poyang Town, boats sailed down Liberation Street. And still the enemies of the new regime came. Three hundred men banded together on June 25 to strike at the county govern-ment. Their assault was a total failure, with seven attackers killed before the rest fled in panic. That same day, the People's Liberation Army dis-patched soldiers to start the difficult process of rooting their enemies out of the mountains.[37]

The New Order and Its Enemies

Control was clearly of great concern in Poyang. But the problem wasn't confined to the county. Throughout Jiangxi, the Communists saw threats on all sides. In mid-July, provincial party leaders issued a directive on "weeding out traitors." Counterrevolutionaries, the directive noted, were going underground, preserving their military power, and secretly moving throughout the province. As forcefully explained in the *Jiangxi Daily* in August, the new regime sought to punish leaders, not followers. Those who confessed were promised lenient treatment.[38]

In urban centers Jiangxi officers moved on suspected Nationalist intel-ligence organizations. In Jiujiang City, just north of Lake Poyang, security officers arrested a group of Nationalist loyalists, accusing the men of establishing an underground government. According to the security officers who cracked that case, these men had set up a broadcasting station and sent Chiang Kai-shek and the Nationalists dozens of reports concerning political and military affairs. With the Civil War still ongoing, they even coordinated aerial attacks on the city. Jiangxi party leaders, also concerned with the rural order, pressed security officers to work with the People's Liberation Army to pacify the countryside. As they warned, bandits and spies roamed widely, finding shelter in mountainous forests where they stashed away weapons and waited for a chance to attack. In Poyang, bandits ambushed nineteen soldiers escorting three grain barges through one of the county's many lakes. All of them were martyred.[39]

With security a top concern, the Public Security Bureau needed men to help bring order to town and country. By the end of 1949 the province could count on 1,816 officers to investigate counterrevolution in Jiangxi. Some, especially Bureau leaders, had just recently arrived from the north. But most were locals, recruited and trained only after the People's Liberation Army crossed the Yangtze River.[40] Many were holdovers from the old Nationalist regime. Holdover officers were politically suspect, but they were desperately needed. The pacification of the countryside produced huge numbers of criminals. Many of these bandits lurked in the mountains near Lake Poyang.[41]

A first campaign against the largest bandit armies in Jiangxi eliminated tens of thousands of men and captured a massive arsenal of weapons. Subsequent campaigns focused on ever smaller groups of holdouts, men who only attacked when victory was assured, often with popular support that the Communists blamed on superstition and the power of landlords and other class enemies.[42] The first investigation in this book, "Bandits, Big Swords, and the Rebel Scholar," details the rise and fall of one bandit uprising as Poyang villagers tried and failed to oust Communist interlopers. Increasingly, battles such as these were fought by Jiangxi security forces. The People's Liberation Army had to keep on moving, leaving Jiangxi for the far southwest, where they once again encountered fierce resistance.[43]

Back in Poyang Town, the Communists continued to cement their power. On October 1 the new regime hosted a public rally, lighting lamps that night in recognition of the formal founding of the People's Republic of China up north in Beijing. The cadres running the county government moved quickly to institute a system of control. Following the precedent of the departed Nationalists, they divided their newly won territory into districts. The county cadres initially established eight districts but by November, finding these large administrative units too unwieldly, they redrew Poyang into twelve smaller districts, not including Poyang Town. Each district was further subdivided into townships, fully staffed with bureaucrats answering to higher-ups in the People's Republic.[44]

The documents generated by the new People's Government typically referred to Poyang communities by their administrative names. Old County Crossing became the seat of the Fourth District. Fengtian Village was identified as part of the Twelfth Hamlet. The cadres serving as bureaucrats, many recently arrived from the north, used this numerical administrative system to refer to Poyang localities in the documents they left behind. Readers take note: these records, created in a bureaucratic system led by outsiders, were used to create this book.

New China, New Poyang

The Communists invited local representatives from the newly redistricted county to Poyang Town. These representatives, drawn from all walks of life, gathered for the first time in the newly named May 1st Auditorium. There they discussed increasing production and managing local industries.[45] Activists from the countryside also came to Poyang Town, where they received a crash course in basic literacy. The first lesson in their textbook covered basic hygiene, including instructions on keeping their fingernails, noses, and necks clean. Another practical lesson was avoiding dysentery. The students also learned about the history of the People's Liberation Army, and how things would change now that the Communists were the ones calling the shots.[46]

One universally welcomed change was the return of a government that was committed to water control. In May 1950 *The People's Daily*, the party's official newspaper, reported the successful completion of repairs to the dikes surrounding Lake Poyang, securing the livelihood of 360,000 farmers. Using the slogan of "providing work to relieve poverty," county governments mobilized villagers to repair the dikes. On any given day, some 125,000 workers helped complete the project before spring planting. Pressed to "rush for the red flag," workers formed "commando units" to engage in labor competitions. The following month, the paper noted that many bandits had returned to farming after the restoration of local dikes.[47] This return to normalcy, however, only belied even greater transformations to come.

Back when the Nationalists were in charge an undersized, privately run power plant only generated enough electricity to power a small part of Poyang Town for about four hours a night. The plant suffered from constant power failures. The new regime built its own power plant, bringing electricity to their offices. Electric lights soon illuminated May 1st Avenue, now tripled in width to fifteen meters across. Construction started on the county's first movie theater. There were other changes. Ever since the late imperial era, Poyang Town residents had flocked to River Road, home to over twenty teahouses. Teahouse owners set up bamboo couches for customers, who ordered snacks to munch on. But no teahouses could be found in New Poyang, only small stands where citizens could buy a quick cup of tea.[48]

In the countryside, which would not have electricity for decades, much work remained. The Communists moved to bring party rule down to the village level through *campaigns*: mass political movements, directed by work teams dispatched to the countryside. In April 1950 the county began rent-reduction campaigns, starting the process of weakening village elites by mobilizing their tenants to demand lower rents. This was combined with targeted attacks on *evil tyrants*, men who had abused their power as the old Nationalist regime slowly crumbled. This book's second casefile, "Big Tiger, Tyrant of the Mountain," explores the crimes, arrest, and trial of one such accused evil tyrant.

In June the county government launched Poyang's first *land reform* campaign, an intervention into local society far beyond anything even proposed by earlier regimes. During land reform, work teams mobilized village activists to restructure land holdings and give political power to the rural poor. They also helped form *peasant associations*, which would extend the reach of the People's Government down to the grassroots. Work teams ventured into a countryside that had been largely cleared of bandits, but there were still major challenges awaiting the Communists. To start, the bureaucrats running Poyang were vastly outnumbered. In 1950 only 184 cadres worked for the county government in Poyang Town. Almost half of them worked for the Public Security Bureau to help tame the countryside. Nineteen were staffed in the county's Tax Bureau. Another 350 were distributed in the county's twelve rural districts, with most offices staffed with twenty-five to thirty workers. During these early days, the county and district governments did not pay their bureaucrats a fixed salary, and instead distributed grain and cloth rations as needed.[49]

No one was getting rich working for the new regime, but those who threw their lot in with the Communists may have been better positioned as the revolution came to Poyang villages. With land reform underway, the county government was prosecuting anyone who pushed back against rural campaigns, as well as punishing rural power holders for mistreating their neighbors under Nationalist rule. This is exactly what happened in "The Case of the Bodhisattva Society," the third investigation explored in this book. As readers will discover, the criminals behind what security officers called the Bodhisattva Society were brought to justice in a unique legal system. In Poyang the Communists drew on Nationalist traditions, taking over the old Judicial Administrative Section to deal with common criminals.[50] But the Communists also insisted that the administration of justice must be led by the party. Rejecting Nationalist legal traditions as "reactionary old laws," the party passed broad statutes promising severe punishment for counterrevolutionaries and any citizen who defied the new regime.[51] Criminals uncovered during campaigns of rural revolution would be prosecuted in a new system of tribunal courts, which functioned alongside the more traditional court system.

Party Justice, Southbound and Down

The result was a dual-track legal system. Common criminals, including bandits and spies, were tried in the *People's Court*, where sentences ranged from the death penalty and forced labor to public apologies. But land reform and other revolutionary campaigns created a flood of cases against criminal landlords and evil tyrants. For these cases, the county established the *People's Tribunal*. In recognition of the wide scope of the task at hand, county cadres established branch tribunals at the district level.[52] These tribunals, in conjunction with peasant associations, became the "legal executor" of land reform and the party's push into village Poyang.[53] These lower tribunals all answered to the new regime in Poyang Town. As readers will see in this book's final casefile, "Merchant Zha

Goes to Court," this gave the cadres running the county government great power. Just as had been the case for magistrates centuries earlier, the county-chief decided the fates of the condemned.

The four casefiles profiled in this book all occurred in the countryside, but during the late 1940s and early 1950s village China was anything but tranquil. This was especially true once the rumors concerning war with the United States in Korea started circulating. The tales spun by rumor-mongers were wild: The People's Liberation Army had already surrendered, and North Korea had been obliterated by American bombs. The North Korean government had fled into China. Lin Biao, the feisty Chinese general who had led the Communists to victory in the Civil War, had perished in the bombing. Kim Il Sung had committed suicide. American bombs had cowed the Chinese Communists into signing a peace treaty. A People's Liberation Army attack on Taiwan had failed. World War III had begun.[54]

None of this was confined to Poyang, or even Jiangxi Province. The paranoia went all the way to the core of the People's Republic. In November 1950 Mao Zedong asked the top leaders of the Public Security Bureau to move against the enemies he saw everywhere. Within days the Administrative Council and the Supreme People's Court issued the "Directive Concerning the Suppression of Counterrevolutionary Activities," launching a nationwide hunt for enemies of the new regime. By the time the campaign to suppress counterrevolutionaries came to an end in mid-1953, hundreds of thousands of Chinese citizens had been executed.[55]

The Communists seemed to encounter counterrevolution everywhere. To the south in Fujian spies and bandits organized riots, pushed back against tax collection, and spread rumors. They infiltrated government offices, sabotaged production, and murdered cadres. Bandits roamed through multiple counties in Hunan Province to the north. Seemingly without regard for the new regime, they murdered cadres and activists, undermined peasant associations, and organized riots. Spies established secret cabals, placed undercover agents in the new regime, and conducted counterrevolutionary propaganda. In Guilin to the southwest, bandits lobbed a grenade into a general goods store, injuring seven. In Guangxi, one of the last provinces to welcome the new regime, bandits put bounties on the heads of peasant activists, offering a huge haul of grain for would-be assassins.[56]

These hints and rumors suggesting widespread resistance in New China can be found in the pages of *Internal Reference Materials*, a journal distributed to ranking party members. These reports reveal that lurking beneath the pomp and circumstance of the party's marches of liberation lay intense concern over local unrest. For decades this journal provided a rare glimpse into the world of counterrevolution, but this glimpse was slight indeed. Readers of *Internal Reference Materials* were only privy to a basic overview of the evil deeds of the men the party called bandits, evil tyrant landlords, and spies. Who exactly were these counterrevolutionaries, and why did they risk everything to resist the Communists? Why might a Confucian scholar throw in his lot with violent rebels? What drove a farmer to murder a Communist organizer? Could men charged as evil tyrants avoid the new regime's punishment by relying on local superstitions and family bonds? And what happens when the accused is innocent? Let's find out.

BANDITS, BIG SWORDS, AND THE REBEL SCHOLAR

Cast of Characters (in order of appearance)

Frightened Shi: Witness to the Xiejiatan bandit attack
Golden Cao: Bandit turned witness
Zhu Old Six: Zhu Baihua, bandit-general
Xie Old Seven: Xie Dongsheng, bandit-general
Boss Wang: Wang Zhenhai, head of the Hengyong Big Swords
Scholarly Wu: Big Sword turned witness
Fiery Huang: Secondary leader, Hengyong Big Swords
Teacher Chen: Private school headmaster, Big Sword
Daoist Zhang: Big Sword master, from Anhui
General Hong: Big Sword turned witness
Second-Captain Liu: Big Sword
Xu Rong: Head of the Chuanwan Big Swords

Frightened Shi Bribes a Bandit Gang

During the late spring of 1949, the assembled forces of the People's Liberation Army camped on the northern banks of the massive Yangtze River for days. The end of the war was finally in sight. The men on the northern shore fought in service of the Chinese Communist Party against their longtime rivals, the Nationalists, then headed by the "Generalissimo," Chiang Kai-shek. This conflict capped off over two decades of brutal violence between the two sides. The Nationalists had long slandered their enemies as bandits but had never been able to root the Communists out of the countryside. Over the years the Communists, under the leadership of Mao Zedong, had steadily gained in power and eventually crushed the forces of the Generalissimo. Some defeated Nationalist soldiers took to the mountains. Now it was the Communists' turn to call them bandits, lumping them together with the outlaws roaming the hills.

As negotiations between the two sides dragged on, any chance of a peaceful resolution to the war faded. When it became clear that no surrender was forthcoming from Chiang and the Nationalists, the order finally came down. Moving in close coordination, army units crossed the river and began the takeover of the towns and villages lying to the south of the Yangtze River. The Second Field Army swept into Poyang County from the north. At first the soldiers met almost no resistance. But hidden in mountainous forests, fortified in their lairs, dangerous outlaws were not inclined to accept the arrival of the new order. This was particularly true in northern Poyang, where the mountainous terrain far from meddlesome officials long provided ideal dens for hardened criminals.

That made Xiejiatan, a small market town nestled in the mountains of the county's north, an ideal target. For years a gang of bandits holed up in Eastern Mountain Ridge, lying on the border with Anhui Province, had used their distance from state power to raid this and nearby communities with impunity.[1] The collapse of Nationalist authority and the arrival of the People's Liberation Army didn't cause them to change their ways. In what was essentially a barter economy, they were particularly fond of banknotes. Modern banking had been in Poyang for barely a decade, but the Eastern Mountain Ridge men were quick to see the true value of their banknotes.

Frightened Shi, one of their victims, would later testify to the danger posed by these outlaws. Nestled among the documents in a Public Security Bureau investigation into bandit activity in northern Poyang, Frightened Shi's statement offers the rarest of access into the realities of this isolated corner of the countryside. Sadly, his statement is woefully lacking in detail. Did he, like nearly everyone else in the county's mountainous north, rely on his fields to survive? Or was he a humble businessman, per-

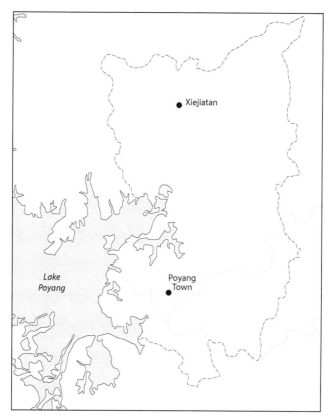

Map 2. Xiejiatan, a market town in the mountains of northern Poyang and the first location discussed in this casefile.

haps running the market's oil press? All we know with certainty is that he had something to lose. To protect his own property Frightened Shi sought out one of his neighbors, a relative of one of the bandits.[2] He pushed a load of crops into the man's hands and pled for the gift to be given to the outlaws with an urgent request to spare his family and his property.[3]

Murderous Bandits Lurk in the Mountains

In official histories of these years, the Eastern Mountain Ridge bandits go unmentioned. Compared to the armies led by Nationalist loyalists, they were little more than small-time thugs. That doesn't make the murders

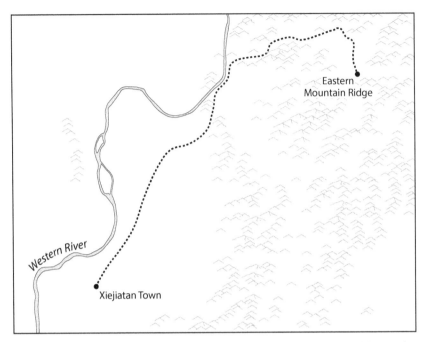

Map 3. The three-hour walk from Xiejiatan Town up to Eastern Mountain Ridge.

they committed any less real. And there were hundreds more of these armed gangs roaming the Jiangxi countryside, preying on their neighbors. The Communists, of course, had been slandered as *bandits* by the Nationalists back in the 1930s. Now it was their turn to vilify these outlaws quickly and uniformly as not only bandits, but also *counterrevolutionary* Nationalist loyalists. Most were simply violent men living off plunder. The newly arrived Communists were merely the latest of their victims.

Long before the dawn of New China, bandits thrived in and around Poyang's lakes, rivers, and mountains. As was the case throughout China during the imperial era, people turned to crime for any number of reasons. Despite romantic tales of banditry as a means to fight corrupt officials, most became outlaws as a means of survival during times of economic hardship. That made a poor county such as Poyang particularly susceptible to banditry. During difficult times some struggling villagers used force to take whatever they could from their neighbors. The thin line between farmer and outlaw meant that, as seen in Frightened Shi's bribe, bandits had connections to their victims. This was especially important when bandits expected to return to farming once an economic crisis passed. As some elders were known to say: "A rabbit doesn't eat the grass around its own nest."[4]

During times of disorder, Lake Poyang and its lucrative trade routes were particularly appealing to the criminally minded. In the years before the Nationalists established their authority, outlaws on and around the lake terrorized merchants and travelers. Some were former warlord soldiers, armed with machine guns and artillery.[5] The arrival of the Nationalists did little to change their ways. The citizens of the county's villages and market towns had long hoped that the Nationalists might one day subdue hated bandits, but the government proved helpless. In fact, as the Civil War went south, officials in Poyang Town twice issued decrees calling for bandit forces to formally join the Nationalist army and help fight the Communists. Poyang outlaws ignored both orders and instead took advantage of the old regime as it collapsed.[6]

Bandits Raid the Xiejiatan Outpost

Because the Nationalists never found a solution for banditry in Jiangxi, Poyang citizens had to find ways to placate or buy off these outlaws. A bribe might save a local such as Frightened Shi. Poyang bandits, however, had no patience for Communist outsiders and took their fight to the new order with force. In the summer of 1949, not long after accepting Frightened Shi's bribe, the bandits from Eastern Mountain Ridge brazenly raided the new government set up in Xiejiatan Township.[7] Their true target, investigators later noted, was a common one among those who attacked the new government or its soldiers: guns.

In this regard the assault was a rousing success. As Frightened Shi would eventually testify, the bandits seized seven guns from the Xiejiatan government offices. A few weeks later they returned, this time with ten men, well-armed with four pistols and a dozen rifles. According to later confessions, including one given by Golden Cao, himself one of the bandit attackers, the outlaws surrounded a small Communist garrison and kept the men trapped inside the government offices for over an hour. Golden Cao and his fellow outlaws called for the Communists to lay down their weapons and surrender. In reply the soldiers defiantly opened fire, starting a prolonged deadlock. Golden Cao's confession reveals a hint of insight into the makeup of the outlaw gang. The bandit leading the siege, fearing his men were not enough, sent his father back to Eastern Mountain Ridge to summon reinforcements. In Poyang, families didn't just farm together, they turned to banditry together as well.

The deadlock was only broken when one of the outlaws threw a makeshift incendiary device made of oil and cloth into the building, setting the structure ablaze. The soldiers, sent south to help create New China, were about to be martyred in the name of the revolution. One attempted to free himself from the blaze by breaking out through a window, only to be quickly shot dead. The remaining men burned to death. From Frightened Shi's account of what happened later that day, the outlaws probably regretted torching the outpost and its contents. Making sure to emphasize that he had no firsthand knowledge of anything, he explained that the bandits didn't depart Xiejiatan until dusk, when they finally returned to their mountain stronghold. The next day locals dug through the rubble, unearthing two rifles and a handgun, all ruined by the blaze. They sent the burnt-up guns to the bandits. Their motivation remains a mystery, but it seems reasonable to believe that the good folk of Xiejiatan didn't want the outlaws to come back in search of any remaining weapons.[8]

Golden Cao Joins Six and Seven

In the aftermath of the murderous raid in Xiejiatan, the continuous arrival of People's Liberation Army forces in northern Poyang made the bandits' lair in Eastern Mountain Ridge untenable. The decision to abandon their longtime holdout must have been a difficult one. They fled east to the mountains overlooking the market town of Houjiagang. There they linked up with two notorious bandit-generals: Zhu Baihua and Xie Dongsheng, known to everyone in these mountains as Zhu Old Six and Xie Old Seven.

Little is known for certain about Zhu Old Six and Xie Old Seven, two major players in this case. In the official history of the county, they are described as reactionaries intent on restoring the old Republic, despite the inconvenient truth that for years the Nationalists had considered both of them outlaws. The loose alliance between the two men, as well as their ability to work with the newly arrived Eastern Mountain Ridge outlaws, suggest they fit neatly into the long tradition of tough guys living outside

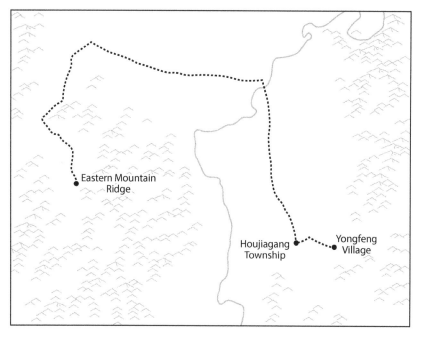

Map 4. Golden Cao and the Eastern Mountain Ridge bandits marched east over three hours to the mountains around Yongfeng Village, not far from Houjiagang Township.

the law. At best, these men were drawn to banditry by the romantic appeal of living outside the law. They also took pride in their own honor and their bonds with other men. But even so, they were quick to violence and valued the ability to inflict pain.[9]

The reports Poyang security officers left behind on these bandits hint at the fluidity of their bonds. Golden Cao, who had taken part in the attack in Xiejiatan, arrived shortly after the rest of the Eastern Mountain Ridge outlaws had already made their way east. As he would eventually explain to his jailors, it wasn't until late June that he paid his respects to Xie Old Seven, acclaiming the bandit-general as his superior. Now pledged to Old Seven, Golden Cao would play a crucial role in the violence to come, linking the earlier raid in Xiejiatan to a larger showdown with the newly arrived forces of revolution. Much blood would be spilled before the conflict came to a close, but Golden Cao lived to tell the entire tale. If the bandit's story can be trusted, of course, is another matter entirely.

A Secret Society Promises Protection

Golden Cao and his fellow outlaws weren't the only ones refusing to accept the arrival of Communist power. Many otherwise law-abiding citizens, fearful of what New China would mean for themselves, turned to their networks to organize resistance. At the village level some rural elites in the northern mountains of Poyang maintained their authority through the Big Swords, a secret society that oversaw large swaths of rural China. This was just one of many secret societies found in the countryside. The first had emerged back in the seventeenth century, uniting some ethnic Han Chinese in opposition to the Qing dynasty, which had been established by "barbarian" Manchus. These underground societies were seemingly everywhere by 1892, when two Sworn Brotherhood Society leaders were arrested in Poyang. The men ran opium dens, which they used as cover for more seditious behavior. According to Qing officials, the men planned on setting the yamen on fire, torching the government offices to start an uprising. Officials executed the two men and placed their decapitated heads on display as a warning.[10] Although, who knows the truth? Saying the men were plotting insurrection against the Manchus was a quick justification for their beheading. The very secrecy of these organizations made them ripe for accusations.

By the 1940s all sorts of secret societies, some of them operating very much in the open, could be found throughout China. These groups defy easy characterization. Some provided complex belief systems through bonds of male loyalty. Others were crime syndicates, focused on profit through vice and other criminal enterprises. At heart, a secret society can be understood as a form of mutual aid. Members were expected to help each other, even if that meant sacrifice. United, members could defend themselves from outside threats. Leaders, meanwhile, were expected to give real benefits to their underlings. Men pledged to these groups embraced alternative forms of hierarchy, based on fictive kinship as opposed to the traditional lineage system that typically dominated Poyang villages. Status, expressed in master-disciple relationships, was often determined by mastery of secret knowledge and participation in the rituals of the society.[11]

Historians have spent years reconstructing the origins and ways of the Big Swords. The society first emerged in Shandong on the North China plain during the 1890s, developing around a martial arts ritual for achieving invulnerability. Practitioners of this ritualized technique, known as "the Armor of the Golden Bell," penned charms on red paper, which they would then burn and swallow. Many Big Sword rituals involved martial arts, laced with fantastic religious practices. Living in a violent society, young men joined the Big Swords to better protect themselves and their communities. Perhaps their faith in the supernatural provided the Big Swords with a mental edge that improved their fighting, which in turn made their claims of invulnerability from knives and swords believable. Talented students traveled to other villages to establish their own Big Sword branches, allowing the society to spread quickly on the Shandong plain and eventually far south to Poyang.[12]

Boss Wang Brings Ghost-and-Monster Tricks to Poyang

By the time the Communists arrived in Poyang, the Big Swords had become a force for order in the unruly and bandit infested countryside. But in official parlance the Big Swords were a *reactionary secret society*. As helpfully explained by the New China News Agency in 1950, these groups were often "headed by spies, landlords, bandits, local riffraff, and hooligans." Rank-and-file members were seen as superstitious commoners, fooled by "ghost-and-monster tricks." The Communists planned to bring order to the countryside by banning any organization led by Nationalist sympathizers and educating the masses through campaigns, with careful attention to suppressing the rumors created by secret society leaders.[13]

In the mountains of northern Poyang any attempt to deal with the purveyors of "ghost-and-monster tricks" would necessarily involve Wang Zhenhai. Originally from Dongzhi County in southern Anhui, Boss Wang had brought Big Sword organization into Poyang in 1945. In just a few short years the organization counted over 200 branches and 4,000 members. Many Big Sword leaders were prominent Poyang men, and some had ties to the Nationalists through their roles in government administration. But initially the Big Swords were a nonpolitical organization, mostly concerned with ritual and self-defense. The arrival of the Communists changed everything.[14]

This was certainly true for Boss Wang. After bringing the Big Swords over from Anhui, he had established himself as the undisputed leader of rural society around Hengyong Township.[15] Part of his power came from his ability to keep his community and the local market safe from bandits like Old Six and Old Seven. But in New China he was now a target, lumped together with the outlaws in the mountains. The arrival of a Communist work team, which set up shop right next to the dam that gave the township its name, must have troubled him deeply. The work team had ventured deep, perhaps too deep, into the mountains to collect grain to feed the soldiers pacifying the countryside and the administrators running the new government. These work teams had been remaking rural life for years. For a secret society leader such as himself, a work team heralded at best a fall from power, at worst a bullet in the head. Boss Wang wasn't going down without a fight. At least he could rely on his Big Sword allies, starting with one of his top lieutenants, a Confucian gentleman with a bum left foot.

A Poyang Scholar Joins the Big Swords

When Boss Wang drew on all his organizational power to move against the work team, he turned to a close ally in the Big Swords, a villager trained in the Confucian classics: Scholarly Wu. As a young student it's probably fair to say that Scholarly Wu hoped that one day he would be remembered as one of the great academic talents of Poyang. He had stiff competition. While Poyang was generally a poor county, its natural resources generated enough wealth to allow many young men an education, and a handful of scholars had achieved great fame. This was particularly true during the Southern Song, when much of North China was lost to "barbarian" Jurchen invaders.

Any account of Poyang scholars of that era must include the famous official Hong Hao, who lived over 800 years before Scholarly Wu. Sent north to the Jurchen capital to serve as an ambassador, Hong was invited to defect and become a high-ranking minister for the Jurchen's puppet Qi state. He refused, and in retaliation the Jurchens kept him captive for fifteen years. His loyalty earned him the highest of praise from the Song emperor Gaozong: "His loyalty pierces the sun and the moon, ambitious but never forgets the lord, his faithfulness is unrivaled."[16] Hong Hao had three sons. Each son achieved the kind of academic success that a Chinese patriarch dare not imagine. His youngest son, Hong Mai, is particularly noteworthy for penning a collection of mystical, fantastic, and supernatural occurrences that ironically provides one of the best records of daily life in the Southern Song.

Poyang continued to produce high-ranking ministers throughout the imperial era.[17] The county's last famed scholar, Zhang Hongzhu, rose to prominence just as the imperial system was faltering. Zhang was a martial scholar, born to a family of farmers and recognized for brilliance in both military affairs and cultural knowledge. His strength and agility made him a natural in the martial arts. After the fall of the dynasty, he returned home to Poyang and took up farming and fishing. One would have to imagine he was deeply concerned with the fate of his homeland when he passed away at the age of sixty-three in 1931. Skilled in archery and deadly with a sword, the talented Zhang Hongzhu would have been an ideal scholar for Boss Wang to rely on as he pondered his options when the Communists crossed the Yangtze and poured into Poyang. Hadn't Zhang engraved four characters on his sword to declare his loyalty and righteousness, as well as his dedication to serving the nation?[18] But Zhang was long dead. Scholarly Wu of Baiyang Village would have to suffice.

In detailed confessions, Scholarly Wu would later insist that he was a reluctant Big Sword. In his mid-forties when he found his world crumbling around him when the Communists came to Hengyong Township, he was by then a man of modest but substantial wealth. Given the difficulties of employment in rural China, he had done well for himself. Scholarly Wu owned land, two pigs, and a water buffalo. He lived in a four-room house with six relatives: his mother, his wife and son, as well as a nephew and his wife and son. To hear him tell it, as he eventually did in ever greater detail to the Communists, whatever prosperity Scholarly Wu had was hard-earned. A scrawny young boy, he developed a bad left foot before he even started his education at a private academy.

This choice of schools made Scholarly Wu a typical Poyang student. Reformers had never quite figured out how to expand educational opportunities beyond private teachers. Even the library they built in Poyang Town toward the end of the imperial era was long abandoned.[19] Growing up in the mountains of northern Poyang, Scholarly Wu studied with multiple private teachers, including Teacher Chen, who had ties to the Big Swords. Students paid for their studies with rice or whatever produce their families could spare. The teaching materials were the standard Confucian classics. Historians would later describe the method of teaching at Poyang private academies as "force feeding" and "cramming." As the saying went: "the teacher speaks, the students listen."[20]

In his early twenties, with financial pressures building, Scholarly Wu became a teacher himself. Over the following decade he largely drifted between teaching and government work. Owing to his own low income and multiple deaths in his family, Scholarly Wu was still struggling to make his way in his thirties. Finally, working with relatives in the Wu clan, he went into business by making full use of northern Poyang's mountainous forests. Peddling lumber and then charcoal, he found financial security. In his telling it was this entrepreneurial spirit, driven by the need to support his family, that made him a potential target of thugs. With bandits like Old Six and Old Seven to fear, how could he resist the recruitment efforts of the Big Swords? As he must have known, a gang of outlaws had even seized Hengyong's humble market in the years before Boss Wang brought the Big Swords to Poyang. In the end he pledged his loyalty to one of the society's elders. As he would later explain to his Communist interrogators, joining the Big Swords protected his home and business.

Boss Wang Calls Two Meetings

Scholarly Wu said he joined the Big Swords in self-defense. But he wasn't just a member of the society, he was one of Boss Wang's most trusted lieutenants. He would have a front-row seat to the secret society's attempt to oust the outsiders threatening their rural order in the summer of 1949. So far, the Communists had a small presence: the armed work team that had set up shop in the government office on the main drag running through Hengyong, not far from the township's all-important dam. Boss Wang moved to mobilize resistance. In late June he wrote to Scholarly Wu, ordering him to gather with other Hengyong leaders in Nantang Mountain for a meeting.[21]

Heavy rain on the day of the meeting kept Scholarly Wu from making it to Nantang Mountain. In his absence, the discussion focused on what might be done about the ad-hoc grain tax that the work team imposed on Hengyong villages. The Communists knew that demanding grain from newly liberated communities was unpopular, but the rapid expansion of the People's Liberation Army as it rolled to victory after victory in southern and southwestern China left the party no choice. Soldiers and bureaucrats had to be fed. Many communities resisted fiercely. In Guizhou, a province lying far to the southwest, the party pushed villagers too far,

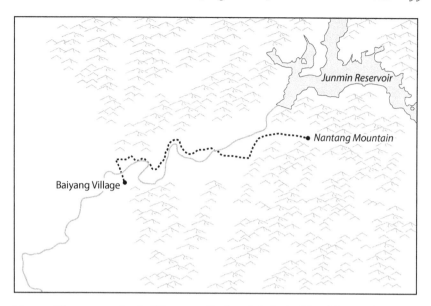

Map 5. The two-and-a-half hour walk that Scholarly Wu didn't make. Note the large reservoir that replaced the Hengyong Dam; the reservoir was built in 1972.

demanding a grain tax that had already been paid to the Nationalists. The result? Farmers, joining with local militias and Nationalist army units, pushed the People's Liberation Army out of twenty-eight counties.[22] Could Boss Wang push the Communists out of Poyang? It would take coordinated action.

About a dozen men from Hengyong Township met in Nantang Mountain that rainy day. Under Boss Wang's leadership they agreed to resist the grain requisition. But how? With no decision made, two days later Boss Wang again sent invitations to village leaders, instructing them to meet for a second time the next afternoon in Huangtupo, right in the heart of Boss Wang's territory.[23] This time Scholarly Wu joined two other Hengyong men and dutifully made his way to Huangtupo for the meeting. Things were moving quickly, but those attending couldn't have known that this meeting would kick off the first of three days of massacres. In fact, one of the two men accompanying Scholarly Wu as he walked to the conspiratorial meeting would be dead within days, shot down by the People's Liberation Army, carrying out orders that Scholarly Wu would wisely weasel his way out of.[24]

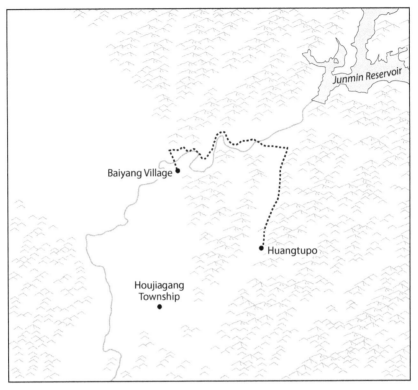

Map 6. Baiyang to Huangtupo, the walk that Scholarly Wu did make for the second meeting. This walk should have taken him over three hours.

This second meeting, held on July 4, 1949, was twice as large as the Nantang Mountain get-together. Many different lineages were represented, with over twenty men in attendance. This included Fiery Huang, another Big Sword boss, who controlled a good chunk of Hengyong villages in his own right. Others were rural elites including Teacher Chen, who ran the private academy. While Boss Wang had called the meeting, the guest of honor was Daoist Zhang, then in his fifties, who was accompanied by two Big Sword masters. The three men, all from Boss Wang's Anhui hometown in Dongzhi County, promised their Poyang brothers that the Communist Party could most certainly be ousted from the county. This, they lied, is what had happened back in Dongzhi, part of an ongoing Nationalist reconquest that was sure to come to Poyang.

From later events, it seems that Daoist Zhang provided the Hengyong

Big Swords with spells and incantations that promised to protect them from harm. Poyang had a rich history of such beliefs. Poyang's own Hong Mai, the Song dynasty scholar, included a few of these superstitions in *Record of Hearsay*, his famed collection of fantastic tales. According to Hong, Daoist priests performed exorcisms in Poyang, sending spirit-generals to pursue and arrest the demons terrorizing their patients.[25]

Scholarly Wu would eventually denounce Daoist Zhang as a fraud. Zhang wasn't even the man's real name. But at this meeting Daoist Zhang had authority, appointing Boss Wang the head of the People's Self-Saving Army.[26] Such a force didn't exactly exist, but the Big Sword men at the meeting seemed determined to start building a military response to the Communists, starting locally in Hengyong. Surprising given the fact that he had no military training, Scholarly Wu was made second-in-command to another Big Sword, General Hong. The two men would eventually confess this and far more to the Communists.

In defiance of the new government that the Communists were planning on installing in Hengyong, Teacher Chen was appointed township-chief. Boss Wang ordered his underlings to mobilize their Big Swords for an assault on the work team that had set up shop alongside the Hengyong Dam. Scholarly Wu left the meeting late that afternoon, knowing the attack on the work team was scheduled for that very night.

Big Swords Attack a Work Team

After the meeting with Daoist Zhang and the Big Sword masters, Boss Wang gathered over seventy of his Big Swords. Boss Wang and General Hong led the men down to the old township offices on the main street near Hengyong Dam. The work team, drawn to the levers of state power, had taken over the building. After the Big Swords surrounded the township office, one man took the vanguard and tried to trick the team into leaving the compound by crying out an alarm: "Bandits are coming!" The work team, not fooled, announced that they would not open the door after dark. Unluckily for them the trickster had a backup plan, exploding a hand grenade that blasted the front door wide open.

Chaos quickly followed. As vividly described in one of Scholarly Wu's confessions, Big Swords swarmed into the government office. The back door flew open as a first work team member ran from the building, only to see Big Sword men everywhere. In the confusion of the moment the work team member made his way to a nearby pigsty where he hid himself away, only to give away his position by firing at the attackers. Seeing the gunfire, Boss Wang tracked him down and knifed him in the back. Grievously injured, the work team member threw down his rifle and stumbled into the fields. He didn't get far. Two Big Sword men followed him and finished him off. Boss Wang gladly picked up the dead man's rifle. [27]

A second man flew out of the compound next, only to be knifed to death, his pistol snatched away by his murderer. With two work team members dead, one of the Big Swords stormed into the compound and dragged another Communist out onto the street, where he sliced off both of the man's ears. He then grabbed the fourth and final member of the work team as he ran from the building. At the order of Boss Wang, Big Sword men executed the two Communists on the spot. With the entire work team brutally martyred, the Big Swords rummaged through their compound, discovering a final rifle. The smoke cleared, and the first day of insurrection went to Boss Wang and his men.

As General Hong would later confess, he and the other Hengyong Big Swords were motivated by economic concerns. Like many with something to lose, they feared the Communists' grain requisition. They had also been told by Boss Wang and Daoist Zhang that the return of the Nationalists was right around the corner. And much like the mountain outlaws who assaulted the Communist outpost in Xiejiatan, the Hengyong Big Swords had been jealously eyeing the guns the work team carried as they went about remaking rural society. Describing the result of the day, Scholarly Wu would later note that Boss Wang and General Hong had taken guns that Xie Old Seven had wanted to add to his own arsenal. The Big Swords, as he put it oddly using the Communists' own rhetoric, had been "liberated."[28] Fresh off their stunning victory, Boss Wang and General Hong may have pondered taking the fight to the Communists. As it happened, the very next day Boss Wang received an invitation to take part in another strike on the Communists, this one in Chuanwan Township, a five-hour march from Hengyong.

Bandits and Big Swords Lie in Ambush
on Pig Mouth Mountain

Boss Wang and his Big Swords were not the only ones dreaming of ousting the Communists from Poyang. Zhu Old Six and Xie Old Seven, holed up in the mountains not far from Hengyong, had been living outside of the law for decades. They had much more to fear than grain requisitions. The bandit-generals might claim connections to powerful anti-Communists, but they were very much on their own in Poyang. The first task of the newly arrived People's Liberation Army was to eliminate men such as old numbers Six and Seven. They were, like it or not, in a life-and-death struggle. The day that struggle truly started was July 5, 1949, just one day after Boss Wang directed the brutal murder of the work team stationed alongside Hengyong Dam.[29]

Familiar with the mountainous terrain, the bandit-generals kept a close watch on the newly arrived Communist forces. It was impossible for them to miss the fact that these outsiders had brought their guns to Poyang. That made the soldiers a particularly attractive target for the gun-hungry outlaws. It was Xie Old Seven who first saw the opportunity to attack when he learned that a small detachment had left the newly established government office in Chuanwan Township.[30] Eight soldiers, each shouldering a rifle, were marching through some nearby mountains to press villagers for grain and would have to travel through the pass at Pig Mouth Mountain. Might this be the perfect spot to catch the soldiers off guard? Xie Old Seven sent Golden Cao and a half-dozen men to meet up with Zhu Old Six, who would lead the ambush.

The Communist detachment, just eight men, was a small one. But they carried eight rifles. To Old Six and Old Seven this must have seemed like a true arsenal. According to a confession later given by their captured allies, at this time the two bandit-generals could only muster two rifles and two pistols between them, a fact that had kept their grand ambitions in check. In preparation for the ambush the bandits gathered all the weapons they could. Golden Cao borrowed four rifles and three pistols from his friends among the Eastern Mountain Ridge bandits. Another bandit ally, originally from Sichuan, contributed four pistols. All told the bandit force consisted of about twenty men. Most, but not all, carried a pistol or rifle.[31] The bandits, while well-armed with their motley collection of guns, wanted backup. Why not team up with their old rivals the Big Swords?

Hadn't the Communists loudly proclaimed all of them to be counterrevolutionaries? As Golden Cao would eventually explain, the bandit-generals reached out to Xu Rong, a Big Sword leader from Chuanwan. Xu had watched the Communists set up shop in his home township. He too was eager to root out the newcomers, and his men from Chuanwan came in force, providing over sixty Big Swords to supplement the smaller detachment of armed outlaws.[32]

The outlaws and Big Swords made full use of the terrain, dividing their forces to set a trap at Pig Mouth Mountain. The Big Sword men played a secondary role, guarding the sides of the road, allowing the bandits to catch the soldiers off-guard. The soldiers never had a chance. Two were tied up and killed on the spot, the other six bound and dragged away. The outlaws later executed five of the six captives, leaving a sole survivor who would yet play a part in this case.

The ambush on Pig Mouth Mountain was a decisive victory for the outlaws and their Big Sword allies. Back in Chuanwan, the newly established government remained in place and well-guarded. But they had just lost eight men, while the bandits had gained eight rifles. Might this be the very moment to decisively crush the Communists? Olds Six and Seven, according to later accounts, believed that their newly acquired guns held the key to further gains against the new regime. They wasted no time, assembling in Yongfeng Village to plan their assault on the government outpost at Chuanwan. They would strike the very next day.

Six and Seven Call on Boss Wang

By shifting the battlefront to Chuanwan Township, the bandits were moving right into Xu Rong's territory. His Big Sword men, having helped successfully ambush the People's Liberation Army at Pig Mouth Mountain, were a natural choice to join the fight. But the bandit-generals tapped into the larger secret society network that interlaced villages throughout these mountains. News moved quickly in Poyang, so perhaps they had heard of how Boss Wang and his own Big Swords had just themselves rooted a work team out of Hengyong Township. What is clear is this: just hours after ambushing the soldiers at Pig Mouth Mountain, the bandit-generals sent word to Boss Wang, telling him to bring his Hengyong Big Swords to join an assault on the new government's base of operations in Chuanwan.

The call to action reached Hengyong that afternoon. The letter was sent to Boss Wang, but news of its content quickly spread to other Big Sword leaders. One of them, Fiery Huang, seemed particularly interested in the offer. The second most powerful Big Sword in Hengyong Township, he had his own ambitions. He must have known that Boss Wang had increased his arsenal at the expense of the martyred work team. The letter's mention of the eight rifles captured during the ambush drove Fiery Huang to act: he hoped to get his hands on some confiscated weapons himself. Without consulting Boss Wang, he quickly gathered over eighty men and rushed to Yongfeng Village to meet up with Zhu Old Six.[33]

Boss Wang, perhaps no longer so desperate to get his hands on Communist guns, took a more measured approach. He divided his Big Swords into two unevenly sized columns, both of which were to meet up with Xie Old Seven. He gave command of the smaller column to Scholarly Wu. Very late that night, when Fiery Huang's men were already well on their way to Yongfeng, seventy-five men, carefully counted by Scholarly Wu, assembled at Han Village.[34] But Scholarly Wu, under orders from Boss Wang to lead these men into battle, went no further. As he would later explain to his jailors, he was no expert in the rituals of the Big Sword Society. He owned not a single gun. And of course he had that bad left foot. How could he be expected to take on the People's Liberation Army? After he took roll at Han Village, he returned home. Some might say it was a cowardly move, but it did save his life.

And so at the crack of dawn the next day the first column of Boss Wang's Hengyong Big Swords, some seventy-five strong, began their march toward Chuanwan, where they would join forces with Xie Old Seven and his outlaws.[35] They were led not by Scholarly Wu but by Second-Captain Liu. Earlier, Second-Captain Liu had accompanied Scholarly Wu to the Big Sword meeting that had preceded the massacre of the Hengyong work team. They were certainly acquaintances, if not friends. Now he stepped in for Scholarly Wu to lead the Big Swords into battle. Boss Wang, sending this smaller force ahead, gathered the rest of his Big Swords into a second column. Boss Wang and General Hong led this main force of over 300 men on a much slower march to Chuanwan. Both columns were to link up with Xie Old Seven and his bandits.[36]

In all, three groups of Hengyong Big Swords marched toward Chuanwan. Fiery Huang had departed first, leading his men to meet up with Zhu Old

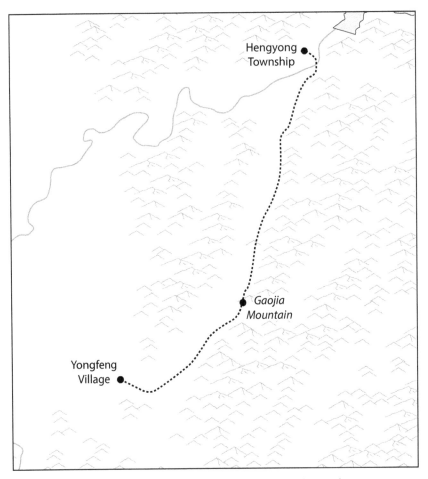

Map 7. Fiery Huang and his men marched over three hours from Hengyong Township to Yongfeng Village, via Gaojia Mountain.

Six. The other two groups were to meet up with Xie Old Seven: Second-Captain Liu led a smaller column, while Boss Wang and General Hong brought up the rear with the bulk of the Hengyong Big Swords. Only the smaller column under Second-Captain Liu, taking over after Scholarly Wu used his weak and sickly left foot as an excuse, would make it to Chuanwan.

Old Seven Has a Plan

For outlaws and Big Swords alike, the old government office in Chuanwan, now occupied by the Communists, was an irresistible target. On a symbolic level the office represented state power. Just as the Communists were drawn to the levers of state power, so too were locals threatened by this new order. And it wasn't just elites who were frightened; many poor farmers, who in fact stood to gain much from Communist rule, were unsure about embracing New China. On a practical level the government building held a stockpile of requisitioned grain. More tantalizing yet were the guns that might further bolster their power in the mountains. But even after losing eight soldiers in Pig Mouth Mountain, the Communists' new government was still guarded by a well-armed force. The bandit-generals planning the assault, having survived for decades in the mountains of northern Poyang, knew this would be far more challenging than the previous day's ambush. According to later accounts, Xie Old Seven personally drew up the plan, a coordinated three-pronged assault, to be launched in the early morning one day after the ambush at Pig Mouth Mountain.[37]

Old Seven's plan called for Xu Rong to lead his Chuanwan Big Swords in a frontal assault on the government offices. Old Seven would lead a second route of attack, aimed at the rear of the district government. He would augment his outlaws with two columns of Big Swords from Hengyong: one led by Boss Wang, the other under Second-Captain Liu. The third prong of the combined offensive, led by Zhu Old Six, was to strike the right flank of the government outpost. Old Six's bandits were joined by Fiery Huang's Big Swords, eighty men drawn from his territory in Hengyong.

Such a plan wasn't necessarily a suicide mission. Just a few months later, a large force of outlaws and secret society men, similarly divided into three assault formations, stormed an even larger target: the government offices in Lichuan, a Jiangxi county lying far to the east. That assault had successfully carried away communications equipment and eighty-nine guns.[38] But Old Seven's plan had a fatal weakness.

Fiery Huang and Old Six Run into Trouble

An impatient man, Fiery Huang had been eager to outpace Boss Wang. While Boss Wang was still mobilizing his men, Fiery Huang quickly marched his own Big Swords to Yongfeng Village, where he linked up with Zhu Old Six. Boss Wang was his elder in the Big Swords, but he was also an outsider from Anhui. Fiery Huang, his allies would later suggest, was looking out for himself and was fixated on getting his hands on a share of the stockpile of weapons held in the Chuanwan government offices. After all, he hadn't gotten anything from Boss Wang's martyrdom of the work team back in Hengyong. Early that morning on the last of the three days of massacres, Fiery Huang could be forgiven for congratulating himself. While Boss Wang was miles away, he was leading his Big Swords alongside Zhu Old Six, one of the county's most feared bandit-generals. And then, up ahead as they marched, was Pig Mouth Mountain.

In retrospect it's easy to see how Xie Old Seven had invited disaster when he instructed Zhu Old Six and Fiery Huang to take this road to Chuanwan. The Communists, having dispatched eight soldiers to collect grain, knew very well that the men never returned. With the mountains full of bandits, it wouldn't have been that hard to guess what might have happened to the soldiers. Knowing the route the eight soldiers had taken through the bandit-infested mountains, the Communists dispatched a well-armed force to find their missing men. Their search took them right to Pig Mouth Mountain.

And so it was that Zhu Old Six and Fiery Huang's column, planning to assault the right flank of the Chuanwan government compound, unexpectedly ran into the People's Liberation Army at the same spot where Old Six had ambushed the eight soldiers just a day before. To be sure, the outlaws and Big Swords constituted a sizeable force. Zhu Old Six led thirty armed men, and Fiery Huang had another eighty carrying rudimentary weapons.[39] The encounter, a surprise on both sides, led to confusion and chaos. Seemingly desperate to break through the impasse, Old Six decided on a direct and, for him, safe course of action. Old Six sent his own men scrambling up the mountain to provide cover fire for the Big Swords, who now served as the vanguard. The men of the Big Sword Society, almost certainly all farmers, had no military training. What they did have were incantations and spirit talismans. While the confessions and reports from the casefile say little about these superstitious beliefs, it seems Daoist Zhang had given these incantations and talismans to the Poyang Big Swords, alongside assurances that they held the power to make the men invulnerable to bullets. And so they rushed forward screaming, "Kill!"[40]

For decades Big Sword masters had taught their disciples that their martial arts training, combined with simple spells, made them impervious to harm. The Poyang Big Swords were no different. Believing themselves invincible, their charge was as foolish as it was ferocious. The soldiers of the People's Liberation Army, firmly entrenched in their positions, quickly set up four machine guns, which they used with devastating results. In an instant eight of Fiery Huang's Big Swords were dead, and over twenty others wounded. Neither the soldiers nor Zhu Old Six's outlaws suffered any injuries. The carnage quickly disabused the remaining Big Swords of their invulnerability. When Old Six called for another charge, the secret society men, having suffered mightily and without any real training, refused orders and instead wisely fled for their lives. Unable to advance in the face of machine guns and without the Big Swords to charge ahead, Old Six and his men had no choice but to turn tail and run. There would be no assault on the Communist outpost's right flank.

Retreating home to Hengyong, Fiery Huang and his remaining Big Swords passed through Gaojia Mountain. There they unexpectedly ran into over 300 Big Swords, led by Boss Wang, General Hong, and Daoist Zhang. Boss Wang and his men were taking a rest far from the battlefront, seemingly in no particular hurry to get to Chuanwan. Seeing Fiery Huang and his injured men, and hearing of the deadly machine guns blockading the road ahead, Boss Wang's Big Swords abandoned their long march. Knowing the day was lost, Boss Wang returned home, his main Big Sword force dispersing in all directions without having even made it close to Chuanwan.

Old Seven Disregards the Odds in Chuanwan

Xie Old Seven, the supposed mastermind of the assault, should have known better. He had been counting on reinforcements from Boss Wang to back up his gang of outlaws. But only the smaller column of Hengyong Big Swords, led by Second-Captain Liu, actually made it to Chuanwan. Boss Wang and the main column of Big Swords never materialized. As for the attack on the right flank, did Xie Old Seven know that Zhu Old Six and Fiery Huang had run into trouble? They certainly never showed up in Chuanwan.

Despite losing most of his Big Swords before the assault even began, Xie Old Seven impulsively pushed ahead with what remained of his plan. Given the Communists' superior firepower, the assault on the Chuanwan government office was always a longshot. Without Zhu Old Six and his men, to say nothing

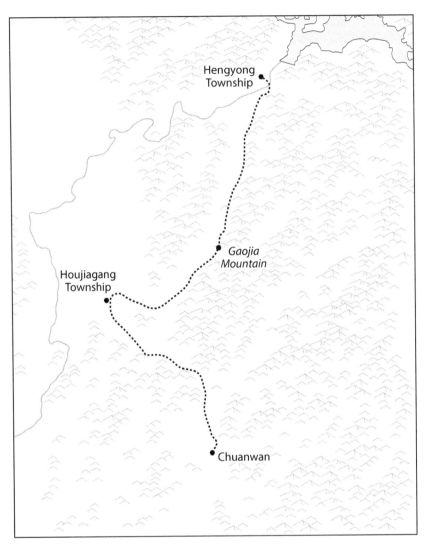

Map 8. Gaojia Mountain, where Fiery Huang's defeated men ran into Boss Wang's Big Swords. This entire journey takes about five and a half hours, but only the Big Swords under Second Captain Liu made it all the way from Hengyong to Chuanwan.

of the hundreds of Big Swords under Boss Wang, it was a suicide mission. This was especially true for Xu Rong and his Chuanwan Big Swords, who took heavy losses as they attempted to storm the front of the government building. According to multiple confessions detailing the massacre, two or three Big Swords were killed while an unknown number were injured.[41]

Xie Old Seven, meanwhile, led eighty men including seventy Big Swords under Second-Captain Liu, who had stepped in to replace Scholarly Wu. Their assault on the rear of the government offices was also a total failure. The men were spotted by a sentinel who quickly and loudly reported the arrival of bandit forces. As defenders opened fire on the attackers, the Hengyong Big Sword men, unaware of the massacre on Pig Mouth Mountain and still believing themselves invulnerable to gunfire, launched a brave but suicidal charge. They managed to kill one defender, but once again machine-gun fire took a deadly toll. Three Big Swords lost their lives, including Second-Captain Liu.[42] At least fifteen others were injured, and the remaining Big Swords, seeing their brothers savaged by People's Liberation Army guns, fled in panic. Knowing the battle had already been lost, Xie Old Seven withdrew with his forces. His outlaws, like those under Zhu Old Six, had sat back while their Big Sword allies threw themselves into machine-gun fire. They would live to fight another day.

The New Regime Seeks Out Ringleaders

After their devastating defeat, the Big Swords could only return home and await their fates under the Communists. Luckily for the vast majority of these villagers, the new regime didn't seem particularly eager to investigate and prosecute the hundreds of men who had marched on the Chuanwan government outpost with murderous intent. It was much more convenient and politically on-message to instead blame counterrevolutionaries for numbing the minds of the peasant masses with superstitious tales and rumors of the Nationalists' imminent return. As one Public Security Bureau summary report described the massacre at Chuanwan: "The Big Sword Society, organized by the ordinary people, saw people dying and understood that their gods cannot be believed, and that very day they refused to follow commands and returned to their homes."[43] This desire to downplay the role of the masses dovetailed nicely with the decline in the power of the Big Swords after the Chuanwan massacre.

The new county government instead focused its ire on the ringleaders: Zhu Old Six, Xie Old Seven, and Boss Wang. In the immediate aftermath of the failed assault the two bandit-generals gathered their men, still unharmed despite the heavy losses among the Big Swords, and retreated to the mountains to return to their lives as outlaws. As the original investigation ended, Old Six and Old Seven remained on the run. Security officers noted that the bandits and their guns uneased the residents of Poyang, who were anxious for the men to be arrested. It would not be easy. As one officer noted, they were "masterful in the ways of banditry."[44] High praise indeed.

Boss Wang hit the road. As the man who brought the Big Swords into Jiangxi, Boss Wang was ultimately responsible for the casualties among the Hengyong Big Swords: eleven dead and over fifty wounded. He abandoned not just Hengyong Township but Poyang County and Jiangxi Province as well. In the aftermath of the massacre, many family members of the dead and injured sought him out, looking in vain for compensation for their losses. Boss Wang, knowing he had led many Poyang men to death, had slunk back across the border to Anhui.[45] Most likely Daoist Zhang and the two Big Sword masters joined him on that return trip home.

During their investigation, Poyang security officers did their best to track down the origins of counterrevolution in the mountains. They took statements from victims such as Frightened Shi, who reported all he knew about the initial murders in Xiejiatan. In his statement, taken by security officers and filed away in the county archives, Frightened Shi noted that most of the bandit leaders from that first incident had been captured in a neighboring county. He emphasized that he was merely an innocent victim with only secondhand knowledge of these facts and never saw anything himself. As to how many people there were, or how many guns they had, he had no idea, having only heard about things after the event. As he stated with force, he was only repeating "what I have heard other people say, I certainly didn't see any of it."[46] He promised, in closing, that if he wasn't speaking honestly, he would welcome severe punishment from the government.

It wasn't just the victims speaking out. Outlaws and secret society men turned on their bosses, saving their own hides and providing inside details into the massacres. Some, knowing that escape was impossible, turned themselves in for what the Communists called *training*: imprisonment, combined with forced labor and ideological education. Three prisoners provided the bulk of information regarding the multiple acts of violence against the new regime, producing multiple confessions, some of them signed by all three men.[47] The first was Golden Cao, the bandit who had pledged himself to Xie Old Seven after getting pushed out of Eastern Mountain Ridge. The second was General Hong, who had accompanied Boss Wang on his leisurely march to Chuanwan. But of the three men who turned on Boss Wang and the bandit-generals, the most detailed confessions came from Scholarly Wu, a literate man with much to answer for.

A Scholar Pleads for His Life

As Scholarly Wu explained in multiple confessions, he had joined the Big Sword Society to protect his business activities. This created a new set of problems as he faced questions concerning exactly how he made his money. With the Communists now running things, the kinds of everyday exploitation that ran rampant under the Nationalists were now considered immoral if not criminal. As a result, Scholarly Wu's narration of his life emphasized his early poverty and hard work. He had become a teacher at the age of twenty just to make money. An early stint working on household registration for the Nationalist government ended when he had to resign after his mother fell ill. While he was teaching at a private school in his late thirties, his father's death nearly threw his family into bankruptcy.

In Scholarly Wu's telling, he originally had a shoddy house, so his relatives took pity on him and gave him a share of their communally held mountain forests, which he used to build himself a new home. He then sold the remaining lumber for a large profit and used that money to purchase his farmlands. Yet he also was forced to admit that his current wealth was the result of exploiting his workers through low pay. Many of these exploited laborers were in fact his own relatives.

Scholarly Wu also admitted to corruption while serving in the now-disgraced Nationalist regime. This included a brief stint as the Hengyong township-chief in 1944. Appointed by the Nationalist county-chief, he only served four months as township-chief before getting booted from office.[48] This dismissal, unexplained in his confession, did little to slow down his political career. The following year he was selected as a local representative. When a new county-chief sent an official to press for grain, Scholarly Wu finally found a way to make politics pay. While in Hengyong, the visiting official swindled a local out of a huge haul of cash. Scholarly Wu knew all about the grift and used his standing to press the outsider to hand over about half of the money, which he greedily kept for himself. And as he now admitted, in recent years he truly led the life of a wealthy local gentry, living the good life without ever really working.

Scholarly Wu admitted to being a stereotypical member of the rural elite, but he made sure to distance himself from far more serious charges at every turn. Exploiting the masses and working for the Nationalists was one thing. Executing work team members and soldiers was something else entirely. In one confession, he carefully explained how he turned down Boss Wang's request to lead a column of Big Swords to Chuanwan: "I had never studied the ways of the Big Sword Society, and I didn't have a gun, and my left foot was ailing, so after taking roll call for the seventy-five men I went home."[49] He made sure to note how little he knew about what happened to the outlaws and Big Swords fighting under Zhu Old Six: "When they got to Pig Mouth Mountain, they ran into the People's Liberation Army and got into a fight, and that's all I know about that." Indeed, Scholarly Wu was insistent that his testimony was almost all hearsay. Above all, Scholarly Wu emphasized how he had been transformed by the largess of the Communists, who had very graciously sent him to labor and study in a prison camp.

Three Men Get the Poyang Prison Blues

Scholarly Wu was one of the first Poyang citizens to experience the Communists' unique blend of reform and punishment. He soon had company. Lots of company. The campaign against bandits, followed by campaigns targeting evil tyrants and other enemies of the revolution, created a surplus of prisoners in the countryside, far more than the county jail in Poyang Town could possibly handle.[50] Poyang's prison-camp system was, in some ways, a direct and practical response to the problem of housing criminals such as Scholarly Wu.

According to one of his many confessions, Scholarly Wu was first arrested by his township government in the aftermath of the failed assault on Chuanwan. In late November the township handed him over to the People's Liberation Army for "training." After being locked up by a military regiment for eight days, he was sent to the Fuliang Military Region Security Section, where he was detained another thirteen days. He was then sent back to Poyang, where he ended up in a prison camp.[51] The last trace of Scholarly Wu found in the casefile finds him there, along-side General Hong and the outlaw Golden Cao. The three men regularly made statements to help clarify just what went down in the mountains of northern Poyang. Sorting everything out took months. Officers were still investigating matters well into the summer of 1950.[52]

In prison camp the three men would learn just how the Communists drew on China's rich tradition of forced labor. Ancient emperors, unrestrained by gods or laws, had mobilized millions by force to build huge projects including the Great Wall and Grand Canal. The Communists established prison camps as early as the 1930s, pressing counterrevolutionaries to make straw sandals and other simple handicrafts. These prisons were dwarfed in size by the camps established after the founding of the People's Republic. In one estimate, as many as 6 million Chinese citizens were sent to labor in prison camps during the first years of the regime.[53]

In Poyang the foundations of what the Communists called *labor reform* were first laid at the start of 1950 with the establishment of the Poyang New Life Camp. The three prisoners were most likely among the very first to labor in the camp, which was soon renamed as the decidedly less hopeful Poyang County Public Security Bureau Labor Reform Unit. At that time, the labor camp housed dozens of criminals, divided into a handful of production units. Prisoners spent most of their time grinding and processing grain by hand. They also opened up land for cultivation, transported lumber and stone materials, dug wells, repaired roads, ground bean curd, and raised pigs.[54]

As Scholarly Wu exited the historical record, his final words praised the positive results from his time in prison camp. "I have received leniency from the government," Scholarly Wu enthused, "which has placed me in a camp to study for over a month. Both my spirit and ideology have made progress. I now understand that my old self-interested and selfish attitude, only caring about good food and good clothes, was entirely wrong." The hopeful closing of his last statement suggests that he was about to be set free: "In the future I will completely correct my former misdeeds. When I return home I will abide by the eight oaths of the district government, and will absolutely not repeat my crimes. Physical labor will be my principle, following the law will be at the core of my heart."[55]

A Scholar Confesses

I will take this opportunity to offer up my own confession: I have no idea what became of Scholarly Wu. If we take his final statement at face value, engaging in physical labor had indeed reformed his ways and prepared him for life in New China. Or perhaps he drew on his experiences in Poyang private academies, when he memorized lengthy Confucian texts, to recite what his teachers wanted to hear. He, like all the confessors whose voices are found in this book, did his best to blame others and make himself look as innocent as possible. But his promise to abide by the eight oaths of the district government suggests he was about to regain his freedom, vindicating his refusal to follow Boss Wang's orders. As to what happened to his fellow confessors, did they get out of that prison camp alive? There is no way to know for certain. The casefile used to write this chapter contains no further clues to their final fates. This is the first problem I faced as I struggled to understand exactly what transpired in the mountains over the course of these three days of violence: the documents are incomplete and so much is left unsaid. What exactly did the Big Swords believe as they rushed toward machine-gun fire? Because security officers dismissed Big Sword practices as backward superstitions, they had no interest in investigating or explaining how the farmers came to believe themselves impervious to harm.

But that's far from the only information missing from the casefile. Take, for example, the unresolved fate of the bandit Golden Cao. In one of his solo confessions, Golden Cao offered up a tantalizing detail concerning the aftermath of the ambush of People's Liberation Army soldiers on Pig Mouth Mountain. Most of the soldiers who liberated Poyang were from the far north, but of the eight soldiers, one was an Anhui man. Compared to the northerners he was practically a local. According to his confession, Golden Cao personally released the soldier as the other seven were brutally executed in the mountains. Did this act of mercy for the soldier save his own life?

Perhaps it did. The Communists were mostly interested in the ringleaders of the uprising, especially Zhu Old Six and Xie Old Seven. The last trace of them in the casefile was that warning that bringing these masterful bandits to justice would be a true challenge. But in the end they were no match for the Communists. In the official history of Poyang, Old Six and Old Seven were captured alive, right in the heart of Boss Wang's old territory. In this account, they were leaders of a Nationalist counterrevolutionary army.[56] In the documents found in the casefile in question, Old Six and Old Seven are occasionally called "bandit spies," but there is no clear evidence that directly links them to the Nationalists.[57] They had been outlaws, of course, long before the Communists ever showed up.

And here is the second problem. During the revolution, words became weaponized. A *bandit* wasn't simply an outlaw who needed to be brought to justice, but a *counterrevolutionary* threat that had to be exterminated. The Communists didn't invent any of this. Like many aspects of life in New China, there were direct precedents from the old Republic. The weaponization of daily language started with the Nationalists, who for decades slandered Communists as bandits. Now it was the Communists' turn to link their political rivals with banditry, erasing the line between outlaw and Nationalist. As security officers investigated this case, Boss Wang also became a Nationalist loyalist, willing to sacrifice everything to revive the old Republic. According to one confession, after overseeing the brutal murder of the visiting work team, Boss Wang immediately planned to strike at the Communist outpost in Stone Gate Street and link up with Nationalist loyalists.

Were Zhu Old Six and Xie Old Seven fighting for the Nationalists? They were certainly fighting against the Communists. And like so many borders during those years, the line between outlaw and Nationalist was in fact thin and permeable. Readers may recall that Golden Cao started this story as one of the Eastern Mountain Ridge outlaws. Back in 1940 the biggest Eastern Mountain Ridge bandit was another Cao, who went by the colorful name Hemp-Skin. Perhaps a close relative of Golden Cao, Hemp-Skin terrorized the countryside along the Jiangxi-Anhui border until 1944, when he recognized Nationalist control by accepting what they called *revision*. Here, it seems, is hard evidence that outlaws were aligned with Chiang Kai-shek. But in a couple of years Hemp-Skin Cao returned to his criminal ways. One year before the Communists arrived in Poyang, he led a small army of bandits and raided the Nationalist government offices at Huanggang Township, making off with guns and thoroughly ransacking local businesses. They even abducted the owner of an oil press. Hemp-Skin Cao and his men demanded a bounty of gold for his return but found it easier to kill the man sent to pay off the ransom. For good measure, they kept the gold.[58]

Olds Six and Seven never revised their ways before the Communists showed up in 1949. They were always outlaws. But that now made them Nationalist loyalists as well. Their easy transformation from murderous outlaws to staunch defenders of the old Republic demonstrate a simple fact about life in the People's Republic. The Communists made sure to label every Chinese citizen. Most citizens were classified as laborers and friends of the revolution. These were the peasants and workers, the honest masses the party could rely on moving forward. But some were classed as counterrevolutionaries: enemies of the new regime who had to be eliminated if the masses were ever to find liberation. These were the bandits, evil tyrants, criminal landlords, and spies. The labels the party handed out were often ill-fits for the citizens who endured them, but all too often the label mattered more than the reality. And as we will see in the following investigation, class labels and the very identity of the accused could easily change to match the needs of the moment.

CASEFILE 2
BIG TIGER, TYRANT OF THE MOUNTAIN

Cast of Characters (in order of appearance)

Comrade Zhou: The primary victim
Comrade Hou: The secondary victim
Hamlet-chief Li: Head of the Thirteenth Hamlet, based in Dayuan Village
Big Tiger: Neighborhood-chief in Fengtian Village
Ms. Zhao: Big Tiger's mistress
Li Number Three: Ms. Zhao's ex-husband
Filial Zhou: Comrade Zhou's son
Chairman Huang: Chair, peasant association
Officer Shi: Interrogation Section officer
Judge Jiang: Jiang Beiran, Poyang county-chief

An Outsider Comes to Dayuan Village

Comrade Zhou wasn't born in Poyang. He only died there. His assassins got to him and his unlucky companion in the middle of the night in Dayuan, a small village tucked deep in the county's mountainous north. Brutally murdered during the violent summer of 1949, he hailed from Duchang, the county situated directly to Poyang's east. Back in Duchang he came from a family of carpenters. In the parlance of the time, he was of the working class, which might explain his attraction to the Communists and their call to fight not just imperialists, but class enemies as well.

As his bereaved son would later explain, Comrade Zhou joined the Communists' cause only months before his murder. He signed up with the People's Liberation Army not as a soldier, but as a *cadre*, a political worker. Comrade Zhou followed the army into the mountains of northern Poyang, where he served in various administrative posts from his detachment's headquarters, then based in Stone Gate Street. His work took him deep into the mountains, directing the collection of the grain tax that followed in the wake of the People's Liberation Army. Already far away from his home in Duchang, Comrade Zhou traveled ever deeper into the Poyang countryside, visiting villages to organize the collection of what amounted to an ad hoc grain levy imposed on wealthy landholders.[1] The outsider quickly made enemies in Poyang. Because those who disliked his message included powerful and wealthy men, Comrade Zhou traveled with the mysterious Comrade Hou. Little can be said with certainty about Comrade Hou, but he seems to have been a security officer, sent in recognition of the danger inherent in the mission.[2]

In the summer of 1949 the establishment of the county's Second District at Tianfan Street brought the pair's grain requisition tour to Jiantian Township. From there they journeyed into the mountains to the north, finally arriving at Dayuan, the village that headquartered the township's Thirteenth Hamlet.[3] Comrade Zhou, a newcomer to political work, followed the party's established practices of rural revolution. As he must have known, one of the surest ways to get wealthy villagers to hand over their hidden grain was to turn their poorer neighbors against them. By mobilizing the power of the peasant masses to press wealthy landlords to hand over grain, Comrade Zhou planned to educate villagers while simultaneously helping feed soldiers, now on the frontlines and far from home themselves. It was time for a *mass meeting*. The Communists had long used these public rallies, full of spectacle and ritual, to rally Chinese citizens.

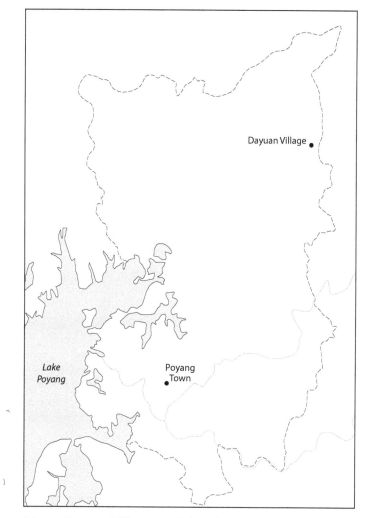

Map 9. Dayuan Village, nestled in the mountains of northern Poyang, and the scene of the crime at the heart of case-file 2.

A Mass Meeting Frightens Powerful Villagers

Hoping to rely on the power of the rural masses to fulfill the order, Comrade Zhou worked with hamlet-chief Li, the man nominally in charge of local villagers, to organize a mass meeting to announce the collection drive.[4] Who else could he turn to? What limited power the party had in Poyang essentially stopped at district government offices. In 1949,

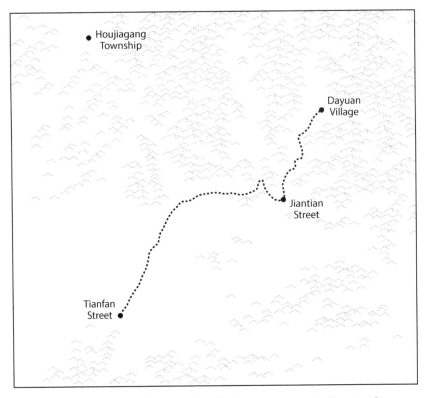

Map 10. Tianfan Street (home to the district government), Jiantian Street (home to the township government), and Dayuan Village (home to the hamlet government). This walk takes over six hours to complete.

the year of Comrade Zhou's murder, there were only eighty-one party members in the entire county.[5] And the mass organizations that the Communists relied on to manage local society were still months away from being established. A man such as himself, venturing into the countryside to promote revolution, was courting danger. He could turn to hamlet-chief Li for assistance, but the man owed no loyalty to the Communists. If he didn't have ties to the previous regime, he certainly had bonds to the extended Li family.

At the rally to press wealthy villagers for grain, Comrade Zhou cast suspicion on local landlords, claiming that they had guns. It worked. The mass meeting was a success, resulting in the call for one landlord to hand over a huge stockpile of grain, five times more than Comrade Zhou had been seeking. With a handful of families holding so much grain, some hungry farmers must have found Comrade Zhou's revolutionary messages appealing. But for elites, his arrival in Dayuan may have brought to mind the warning found in *Outlaws of the Marsh*, the classic tale of banditry in the countryside: "Fear not officials—except those who officiate over you!"[6]

Comrade Zhou was an outsider in Poyang, with no ties in Dayuan. And even as he rallied villagers against their wealthier neighbors, he only had one man, Comrade Hou, to protect him. Some villagers responded to his call to seize the grain of wealthy landowners, but the Communists had zero party presence in these mountains. What happened next might have been expected. Maybe he should have known better, but Comrade Zhou was still new to rural revolution. Angry and fearful that Comrade Zhou was turning their poorer neighbors against them, local elites pushed back with deadly force.

And so it was that on the night of July 8, 1949, eleven men made their way through Dayuan Village, walking the dark but familiar paths with a new purpose.[7] Later reports would say they were "ruthless and lacking in conscience." These men, however, were a far cry from the well-armed bandits that had ambushed Communist soldiers as they attempted to traverse Pig Mouth Mountain just days earlier. Despite Comrade Zhou's claim that the forces of counterrevolution in these mountains were well-armed, the men making their way through Dayuan carried no guns. Instead, almost all of them brought little more than spears. Their leader, a local strongman from a neighboring village, brandished a saber. Then in his early thirties, his neighbors knew him by his nickname: Big Tiger.

Big Tiger Rises to Power

Big Tiger, an important man in the extended Li family, was in his early thirties when the Communists brought their liberation to Poyang County. He lived in Fengtian Village, just down the way from where Comrade Zhou ran into trouble demanding grain in Dayuan. Big Tiger had a rudimentary education, only lasting a few years at a local school. By his early teens he was already working the fields, tending water buffaloes before becoming a farmer. In this he was a typical Poyang man. The county's subtropical climate and fertile soil were ideal for rice paddies, and in

1949 nine out of ten residents engaged in agricultural work.[8] Few truly prospered. The Communists, by attuning their revolution to rural concerns, had come to power through the support of such farmers.

The eldest of three brothers, the youngest of whom was still living at home with their folks, Big Tiger was doing well for himself in the mountainous north. That was largely due to his extended family ties. In Poyang, clan influence affected nearly all aspects of village life. His family owned property, including plots of abundant Poyang forests. Wealth brought power, making the Li clan locally dominant, rivaled only by the Huang lineage. Together the two families ran things in this mountainous corner of Poyang. As for Big Tiger, his own fields and housing were all inherited from his parents. Together with his paternal male cousins he owned ample housing and land, a full set of agricultural tools, a water buffalo, and even a grove of fir trees in the mountains.

Big Tiger would one day be condemned as a *landlord* and an *evil tyrant*. He had, by his own account, helped murder a cadre. But even according to the standards of the new Communist regime, he was no landlord. By definition, landlords didn't engage in any labor, and instead lived off exploitation, typically by collecting rent and giving out high-interest loans. Big Tiger, conversely, was a farmer. By engaging in agricultural production, he should have been labeled a *peasant* under the party's class system. As he would later try to explain to his jailors, "my family and friends are all peasants."[9] In the months before committing murder, he continued to farm, bringing new land under cultivation to grow corn and wheat. Still, thanks to his family connections he was relatively wealthy. These ties to family wealth, as well as his sizeable frame, weren't the only reasons for Big Tiger's power among his neighbors. Before the Communists arrived, Big Tiger served as the *neighborhood-chief* in Fengtian Village for four years.

Big Tiger Collects Taxes

Starting in his late twenties, Big Tiger played a small part in the *baojia*: the hamlet-neighborhood system, an administrative network of control that had been long imagined but rarely implemented. This last incarnation of the system in Poyang dated back to 1930. That year, just as the Nationalists were brutally suppressing a premature Communist revolution, the Poyang countryside was divided into a numerical administrative system. Households were grouped together to form a *neighborhood* unit. Multiple neighborhoods formed a *hamlet*, and multiple hamlets created a *township*. According to Nationalist administrators in 1948, the county counted 37 townships overseeing 468 hamlets, which in turn oversaw 4,493 neighborhoods.[10] Each of these neighborhood units, most of which consisted of a single village, would have an unpaid chief such as Big Tiger in charge. Here's what that administrative structure looked like for Big Tiger before the Communists came to power in his corner of the countryside:

Poyang County

↓

Jiantian Township

↓

Thirteenth Hamlet (based in Dayuan Village)

↓

Big Tiger's Neighborhood: Fengtian Village

The Nationalists didn't invent any of this. As an administrative ideal, the hamlet-neighborhood system of controlling local society dates back to the dynastic era.[11] Imperial and Nationalist states had little interest in directly intervening in local affairs, preferring instead to maintain basic order and collect taxes. For these limited purposes, the hamlet-neighborhood system sufficed. True, even in these most basic functions, the system never achieved anything near the results imagined by imperial or Nationalist planners. Any grander ambitions were merely dreams. Looking at the system's ability to maintain water-control projects, one historian deemed the system "largely a shell with little substance."[12] But by linking rural communities with the county government, the hamlet-neighborhood system became an inescapable part of life in Poyang villages.

Big Tiger's main role as neighborhood-chief was collecting taxes from his fellow villagers in Fengtian. In Poyang, as was the case throughout the Chinese countryside, collecting taxes often meant engaging in corruption. Outsiders have long seen the corruption built into the collection of rural taxes as a sign of moral decline, but in truth some grift was necessary for the system to work. Collecting taxes was a burdensome and onerous task. Wealthy families often refused to take responsibility for taxing their neighbors, while poorer men lacked the authority to enforce payment. In the imperial era, the job often fell to yamen runners, who added fees for the expenses they incurred while they traveled about collecting taxes.[13] As long as the job of collecting taxes remained unpaid, as it did during the era of Nationalist rule, tax collectors found ways to enrich themselves. There was little reason to take on such a burden besides the promise of benefiting from a bit of small-time corruption.[14]

Big Tiger never explained how he came to take the post, but he eventually admitted to using this minor position of local authority to enrich himself in the expected ways. Whenever he collected taxes for the Nationalist government, he made sure to keep a little extra for himself. He began collecting taxes in 1945, officially becoming a neighborhood-chief in 1946. That year, in celebration of the victory over Japan, the Nationalists reduced taxes. Big Tiger kept that good news to himself and embezzled all the extra grain he collected from his neighbors. In early 1949, shortly before the arrival of the Communists, Big Tiger oversaw a one-time collection to fund repairs for one of the county's few roadways. He used the opportunity to pocket eight silver dollars.[15]

The Neighborhood-Chief Abuses His Power

His indiscretions went beyond petty corruption. In 1946, perhaps not coincidentally right around the time he became neighborhood-chief, Big Tiger, a married man, began an affair with Ms. Zhao. Despite the supposed dominance of Confucian values in the countryside, marital relations in Poyang villages could be quite messy. Domestic violence was widespread, with some shocking assaults making the pages of *The People's Daily* in Beijing.[16] Affairs were common as well. This seems especially true with widows, who were under immense pressure from their dead husbands' families to remain single, regardless of their youth or personal wishes.[17] Big Tiger's lover, however, was no widow. Scandalously, she was the wife of Big Tiger's own clansman, Li Number Three.[18] The affair eventually caused Ms. Zhao to file for divorce, or at least that's how Li Number Three bitterly saw things.

Despite the affair, Big Tiger was a pillar of the local order in the late

1940s. This included a position of importance in his local secret society, but because of the underground nature of the organization, the details of its origins, nature, and even its very name are murky. Some knew it as the Huang-Li Society, the name reflecting the two clans that ran things in this corner of the mountains.[19] In one confession Big Tiger told his jailors he only organized the society in May 1949, just two months before the murder of Comrade Zhou. In another he admitted to having been a mid-ranking member for two years. In yet another, Big Tiger said he had first organized a dozen of his neighbors back in 1941 in order to protect lives and property from bandit attacks.[20]

According to security officers, Big Tiger held a mid-level position of authority in the Huang-Li Society, becoming the "adopted son" of one of the wealthy landlords who ran the organization.[21] The arrival of the Communists should have been good news for Poyang farmers such as Big Tiger, but his ties to the county government and his family made him much more than a typical tiller of the good earth. The new order directly threatened him and the powerful families who ran the countryside. Indeed, one of the new regime's first orders was a call to disband secretive organizations. For the leaders of what security officers called the Huang-Li Society, regime change threatened their hold on the countryside. Outsiders such as Comrade Zhou were feared, especially when they rallied the poor to seize grain. If the Communists could take away their grain, what was next? Their land?

Big Tiger Leads an Assassination Squad

Comrade Zhou, by organizing a mass rally to press local landlords for grain, had made a fatal mistake. These men from the Huang and Li clans, who would later be described as "big feudal bosses," weren't to be trifled with. Three prominent Dayuan landlords, one of whom had been explicitly targeted by Comrade Zhou during the mass meeting, masterminded the murder. The three men met on the night of July 4, 1949, just as Boss Wang was leading his Big Swords in their assault on the work team stationed by Hengyong Dam. Back in Dayuan, the three landlords agreed that the threat that Comrade Zhou's message posed to wealthy villagers such as themselves was simply too great to ignore. This rabble-rouser had to die. The landlords, however, wouldn't be the ones to carry out the actual murder.

Two days later, on the afternoon of July 6, the three conspirators met again for lunch. This time they invited Big Tiger to join them, and over their meal they discussed the plan to rid themselves of the troublesome outsider. Big Tiger would later downplay his ties to the three landlords, but security officers would insist on connecting the men: one of the land-lords was his "adopted father" in the Huang-Li Society. On the evening of July 8 Big Tiger and the assassins gathered in Fengtian Village. Big Tiger mobilized four men, all of them in the employ of his "father" in the Huang-Li Society. Another ruffian, this one from the Huang clan, brought another five men.[22] Most of the attackers came armed with spears. Big Tiger carried his saber.

Leaving Fengtian, Big Tiger and his men made their way up the moun-tains to nearby Dayuan, where they proceeded directly to the house of Landlord Li, the man that Comrade Zhou had singled out in his mass meeting. Landlord Li and Big Tiger tapped into their family network to mobilize other Li men to orchestrate the assassination. That started with the hamlet-chief. Just days earlier, hamlet-chief Li had helped Comrade Zhou organize his mass rally. Now his actions would reveal that his ties with the Li clan and the local order came before any demands from the new regime. Landlord Li's nephew led Big Tiger and his men to the house of yet another Li man, where Comrade Zhou and Comrade Hou were spending the night. If Comrade Hou was in charge of security, he proved little help. He was captured sound asleep, lying in bed beside the man he was supposed to protect. Big Tiger and his men, claiming to be part of a "National Salvation Militia," seized and bound the two cadres. They carried the two men back down toward Fengtian, stopping at a hillside pavilion halfway between the two villages.

It was here, at the Changshun Pavilion, that Big Tiger's men brutally assaulted the two victims with their spears. Depending on who tells the story, Big Tiger may or may not have used his saber to finish off Com-rade Zhou. One of the most zealous attackers stabbed Comrade Hou six times, three of the thrusts aimed at the man's head. In total Comrade Hou was stabbed fifteen times before the assassins walked away, leaving the two men for dead. Later, after Comrade Zhou's daughter came to confirm the identity of his corpse, Dayuan villagers buried the man who had come to bring them liberation.

Miraculously, Comrade Hou survived the assault at Changshun Pavil-

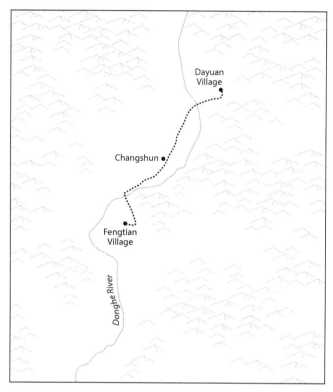

Map 11. Changshun, midway between the one hour walk from Dayuan Village to Fengtian Village.

ion and made his way back to safety. With one of the victims still alive, what happened in the pavilion that night was never in doubt. Comrade Zhou provoked the attack by rallying the masses of Dayuan against their local landlords. Fatally underestimating the power of the Li and Huang clans, he perished that evening beside the Changshun Pavilion, another martyr for the revolution. Everyone knew about the murder, and that Big Tiger and his saber had led the way. But the Communists had yet to establish their new order in this mountainous corner of Poyang. Big Tiger was a dangerous man with strong ties to his rural community. In the aftermath of the murder, with the new regime still fragile, a coalition of local elites and newly arrived cadres decided that Big Tiger and his men should merely be fined.[23] They allotted a payment of grain to Comrade Hou, stabbed fifteen times and left for dead, in compensation for his injuries and to cover his medical expenses. The family of Comrade Zhou, meanwhile, was also promised a load of grain, part of which was intended to cover his burial costs. Big Tiger, going on with his life in Fengtian Village as if nothing had ever happened, seemed in no rush to deliver the grain to his victims.

The New Order Searches for Evil Tyrants

The People's Liberation Army had arrived, chasing away Nationalist soldiers and bandits alike. Cadres roamed the countryside, mobilizing the poor to demand wealthy landlords hand over grain to help protect the new order. Yet the people of Jiangxi continued to push back. In the first half of 1950 the province witnessed eighteen uprisings against the new order. Over 200 cadres and citizens had been murdered, another 55 cadres abducted.[24] And in the mountains of northern Poyang, months after the brutal murder of Comrade Zhou, Big Tiger roamed the streets of Fengtian Village as a free man. The grain he promised the dead man's family was slow to materialize. Could his neighbors have believed that the arrival of the Communists would indeed bring about real change?

In these mountains, far from centers of administration, real change would take time and sustained effort. The Communists had both. First they rid the countryside of the gangs of armed bandits, led by men such as Old Six and Old Seven, that terrorized the new regime. Only then did the county government launch a campaign against feared local strongmen, who would be charged as *evil tyrants*. Some Poyang peasants used these campaigns to press their wealthier neighbors for cash, valuables, or even land. Others used rural revolution to find justice for the kinds of misdeeds that the old regime had long tolerated or left unpunished. Unluckily for Big Tiger, he had an enemy who fell into both camps: the filial son of Comrade Zhou.

Even with the Communists in charge, the Confucian value of filial piety, devotion to one's parents and ancestors, remained central to village life. That gave the martyr's son power. In the aftermath of the midnight assassination, Filial Zhou relentlessly sought justice for his slain father, repeatedly pressing the township administration to prosecute Big Tiger. Almost a year after the murder, campaigns against evil tyrants in the early summer of 1950 provided the perfect opportunity to push the new regime to punish Big Tiger. The charges Filial Zhou leveled against Big Tiger, after all, perfectly matched the Communists' understanding of the worst tendencies of local strongmen during the final years of Nationalist rule.

The "evil tyrant" label was reserved for particularly wicked local powerholders in need of arrest, public denunciation, and trial once villages came under Communist control. The party left the distinction between landlords and evil tyrants vague, leading one party leader to complain about the fluidity of the evil tyrant label, which could be given to a villager who spoke too strongly or cut down the wrong tree, as opposed to someone who had "truly seized an area to bully the masses."[25] In practice, nearly any landlord, especially during the heat of confrontational class struggle, might be called an "evil tyrant landlord."

Most of the men charged as evil tyrants in Poyang were arrested during the 1950 campaign that Filial Zhou used to level his accusations against Big Tiger. But charges were also filed against men who pushed back against the new regime during campaigns to requisition grain, reduce rent, and redistribute land. Cases were usually reported by peasant associations or work team cadres to township or district governments before getting turned over to the legal system.[26] The party was eager to prosecute these men and in theory these trials should have been much welcomed by the masses who suffered under the old regime. But Filial Zhou had trouble getting Poyang folk to arrest one of their own for murdering an outsider from Duchang.

Filial Zhou Seeks Justice

Filial Zhou formally filed charges on May 8, 1950, explaining in the humblest of terms how Big Tiger had led a gang of hooligans to brutally assassinate his father in the dead of night. In his accusation, he drew on Confucian tradition, presenting himself as a filial son in search of justice. But he also described his enemy in weaponized words that vividly evoked the new regime's imagination of village China in the dark days before liberation. According to Filial Zhou, Big Tiger and his men, nearly all from the Li and Huang clans, were in fact members of the Big Sword Society. Big Tiger, he further claimed, was a bandit-chief acting under orders of the "bosses" of a notorious Nationalist loyalist who had terrorized Poyang during the summer of 1949.[27] They had murdered his father, a "revolutionary comrade" who had "served the people." Big Tiger was nothing more than a "counterrevolutionary element" and a "public enemy of the people." Incendiary charges, laced with the dehumanizing labels reserved for those who simply had to be executed.

In his statement, Filial Zhou noted that he had repeatedly reported these crimes to township authorities, who had shielded this counterrevolutionary from punishment. Instead of correctly handling the case, Big Tiger had been set free with the provision that he provide the son with a payment of grain, but as of now, long after his sister had identified their father's corpse, this promise was nothing but "a blank piece of paper." In highly deferential language, Filial Zhou, again reminding cadres that his father had been martyred in Poyang, pled for his own safety while he was away from home seeking justice. He also demanded vengeance for his father's murder, pleading the "honorific" township-chief to "safeguard the people's public good" by arresting and bringing Big Tiger to trial.[28] Despite all the accusations Filial Zhou threw at the man who killed his father, it still wasn't enough. Big Tiger remained a free man for another six months.

Big Tiger, Fake Neighborhood-Chief, Gets Arrested

Even after Filial Zhou demanded justice for his slain father, Big Tiger's reputation and influence among his neighbors had been sufficient to shield him from justice. And he was still a feared man. According to one of his later confessions, it seems Big Tiger wasn't above roughing up newly arrived government officials.[29] No wonder they were in no rush to arrest him. The dead outsider's life would simply be repaid in grain. But Big Tiger was slow to pay his debts. Even if he had paid in full, it was probably inevitable that the People's Government would want more than grain to compensate for the murder of Comrade Zhou. And with a nationwide push against counterrevolutionaries coinciding with a new round of rural revolution in Poyang, the ties to the old order that had protected him were rapidly losing power. The Communists would insist on developing leaders for their *peasant associations*, the mass organizations that now managed village society in New China. The men and women who rose to leadership positions in peasant associations, typically among the most disadvantaged in the old regime, owed their newfound power to the party, not clan loyalty. With Filial Zhou pushing for vengeance, skillfully using the Communists' own rhetoric to force the township government to investigate, Big Tiger's fate was sealed. It was just a matter of time. On the afternoon of December 11, 1950, Big Tiger was finally arrested.[30]

At the time of his arrest, he was still in his early thirties. No mention is made in the casefile as to exactly where he sat in lockup, but prisoners such as himself were kept at local detention centers.[31] Less than two weeks later, on December 22, 1950, Big Tiger made the first of several confessions. It was the start of a long and winding attempt to avoid the executioner's bullet. In this initial statement, Big Tiger was already fighting for his life. Asked to detail the "facts of his crimes," he focused on his days collecting taxes, long before the Communists ever came to Poyang. The precise language he used suggests that he had been denounced at a mass meeting after his arrest. That was to be expected. Security officers regularly brought accused evil tyrants to public rallies, allowing victims to charge them with various crimes and demand justice for past abuses, further legitimizing the new Communist regime as a force for order. Sometimes this backfired. In Huichang County, down in southern Jiangxi, officers learned this the hard way while escorting two men already sentenced to death to a mass accusation rally. Ambushed by bandits, the security officers lost their prisoners, weapons, and their lives.[32]

No one came to Big Tiger's rescue, and there is no direct evidence of his exact experiences at any public trials. But he spoke like a veteran of party justice. Using one of the Communists' favored words for describing the Nationalist regime, he delegitimized his old government post by calling it *fake*. And as his confession made clear, he had heard of his crimes directly from the masses. As he explained:

> In the second month of 1946, because I'm a strong guy, I was made a fake neighborhood-chief, and after I became a neighborhood-chief, each time I requisitioned grain I would always get a little extra and use the surplus to enrich myself. The fake government sent officers and men to the countryside to requisition grain, and I always made sure to carefully follow government orders. I was very strict when collecting and searching for grain.

Big Tiger then made a vague reference to "fake" township soldiers attacking the People's Government. Could this be proof that Big Tiger and his buddies tried to intimidate the bureaucrats sent by the new county regime? He then explained what happened once he got arrested:

As a result of my three years as neighborhood-chief people criticized me, saying I cared only for the fake government and not the people. They also said I was the fake government's dog leg, a hired thug, who worked diligently to coerce the people. When landlords and the masses were liberated, the crimes I committed as a fake neighborhood-chief couldn't be evaded.[33]

Big Tiger also admitted to being a mid-level leader in the Huang-Li Society that ran things in this corner of Poyang, at least until the Communists declared secret societies illegal. And as neighborhood-chief he also had dealings with a previous hamlet-chief. That man, a landlord, had hit the road back when the Communists first arrived in Poyang. Stewing in a detention center, Big Tiger probably wished he had been able to join him on that journey.

Big Tiger Gets a Rich Peasant Class Label

Asked by his jailors to describe his economic status as a citizen of the People's Republic, Big Tiger emphasized his labor. The new regime was dividing rural society between evil exploiters and honest laborers, and Big Tiger knew this gave him an advantage. As was the case throughout the countryside, everyone in Poyang was given a class label. *Landlords* didn't farm themselves, and instead lived off land rents and other forms of exploitation. *Rich peasants* were farmers who also made a profit off the labor of their neighbors. Self-sufficient farmers became *middle peasants*. And the rural poor, owning little or no land, were classed as *poor peasants* or *hired hands*. Farming made Big Tiger a peasant, which in turn made him a potential ally to the Communists. He made sure to note that except for a younger sister who had married into a landlord family, all of his family and friends were peasants. "I have always farmed," he insisted, and indeed township investigators recognized him as a well-off farmer by classifying him as a rich peasant.[34]

To be sure, this wasn't an attractive class label. According to the party's own classification system, while rich peasant households engaged in labor, a significant portion of their income came from exploitation, either through feudal exploitation in land rents and usury, or capitalist exploitation through wage labor and commercial enterprises. As a result, the party had a decidedly negative view of rich peasants. One party leader went as far as to declare these farmers as "selfish" and "full of tricks," looking out for themselves and their narrow economic interests.[35] During the early stages of rural revolution, some poor activists attacked rich peasants, seizing any extra wealth they could locate. By the time the Communists made it to Poyang, however, things had changed. The party now embraced what had been previously dismissed as the "rich peasant line," allowing wealthier farmers to keep all their property and contribute to the rural economy.[36]

It made sense for Big Tiger to emphasize his own labor, drawing a line between himself and true class enemies. Better a rich peasant than a landlord. He also made sure to explain how he was now a model citizen: "After liberation, I continued to clear land for cultivation." Hadn't the northern cadres down in Poyang Town called for increased production? When the peasant association called him to several meetings to ask him to give grain and money for winter clothes, he complied. In his telling he was a humbled rich peasant, handing over what he could to help the poor and respectfully following the orders of the village leadership. As a rich peasant he was excluded from the newly empowered peasant association, but he claimed to be happy with how things were changing: "The other meetings, because I'm a rich peasant, well I never attended. These days Chairman Huang runs the peasant association, and he is very fair and conscientious in how he handles things." As for the old local order, Big Tiger made sure to note that the real power holders had already fled. That included the old "fake" township-chief and his father, both Huang men. "The peasant association has been looking but hasn't found them yet."[37] Big Tiger signed his confession with his given name, identifying himself as a member of the Li clan, and affixed his thumbprint to the document to confirm his identity.

After taking his statement in late 1950, township officials based in Jiantian pushed Big Tiger to reveal the extent of the Huang-Li Society. Big Tiger responded: "I organized the Huang-Li society in the third month of 1941 with about twelve men from local villages. This was done to protect local markets against bandits and to protect life and property." Yes, there had been violence, but Big Tiger made sure to note that he and his men "never beat any good people." When pressed on how he had oppressed the masses, Big Tiger admitted that during his time as neighborhood-chief he had wronged several of his neighbors, while adding that he had done his best to pay them back after Poyang was liberated. "It's true that I oppressed the people, and for this I'm sincerely regretful and promise to do everything I can to change my ways."[38]

A New Accuser Brings Scandalous Charges

Big Tiger, clearly hoping for a second chance, was saying all the right things. And as his trial approached, public opinion was on his side. As reported by township authorities, most villagers wanted Big Tiger imprisoned but eventually released. Many of these villagers, of course, came from Big Tiger's own lineage. In Poyang villages loyalty to family had always come before loyalty to the state. True, Big Tiger had a persistent enemy in Filial Zhou, who had gotten him arrested. But could his neighbors really want him punished for killing a troublesome grain collector from Duchang? Then, while Big Tiger sat in jail awaiting trial, Filial Zhou found an ally in his push for justice, this one a Poyang man from Big Tiger's own clan: Li Number Three. The man's wife, Ms. Zhao, had divorced him after having a lengthy affair with Big Tiger. Now Li Number Three finally had a chance to speak out against the man he blamed for his divorce.

The details of this and other crimes became the focus of a new round of questions for Big Tiger, with the emerging township leadership now handling his case. This included Chairman Huang, the man Big Tiger had praised for his honesty in leading their local peasant association. These new leaders, trained by Communist work teams, weren't inclined to protect Big Tiger simply because he was a local. As the new investigation developed, Big Tiger made a "supplemental confession" on September 28, 1951, almost a year after his arrest. The Fengtian Village native was in trouble. When he was initially brought into custody, he had been accurately classified as a farmer by profession. Now security officers charged him as an evil tyrant landlord. This was exactly the type of accusation that could lead to a death sentence.

As seen in the transcript of his interrogation, Big Tiger was asked to give a "detailed and honest account" of his crimes before liberation and his counterrevolutionary activities after the arrival of the Communists. He again admitted to corruption during his time collecting taxes. Revisiting his role in the Huang-Li Society, Big Tiger took the opportunity to remind his interrogators that the real head of the organization, a landlord from the Huang clan, was now long gone. He also discussed the origins of the plot to murder Comrade Zhou. But reflecting the charges made by Li Number Three, Big Tiger now confessed to a new crime, an adulterous affair with Ms. Zhao. He refuted, however, the idea that he had anything to do with her divorce from Li Number Three, claiming that the married couple had separated only after the affair ended. That couldn't be his fault. He also made sure to note that their divorce had been mediated by the cadres over in the district government. Mysteriously and without any further explanation, Big Tiger added: "I couldn't get married with Ms. Zhao."[39]

Big Tiger is Tried at the Branch Tribunal

After multiple rounds of investigation, it was finally time for Big Tiger to stand trial. As he would discover, the Communist legal system in Poyang now ran along two tracks. On the first track ran the regularized court system, built on the corpse of the old Nationalist justice system: the People's Court. Shortly after bringing liberation to Poyang, the Communists established a full network of people's courts to prosecute regular criminals, including bandits and spies.[40] But Big Tiger wasn't tried in the People's Court system. Like other criminals prosecuted during mass campaigns in the countryside, his trial took place in a branch of the People's Tribunal. Hundreds of such tribunals were established during 1950 throughout Jiangxi at the city, county, and district levels to deal with criminals uncovered during mass campaigns. Poyang County's own People's Tribunal was established in March 1950. While essential to the party's push into village China, these tribunals were disbanded after the campaigns to restructure village life ended.[41]

The first trial against Big Tiger, evil tyrant landlord, was handled by one of the county's eight branch tribunals, established at the district level to handle special cases during the first days of Communist rule.[42] He was charged with a litany of crimes: living entirely off corruption for four years as neighborhood-chief, "seizing" Ms. Zhao from her husband, disrupting rural revolution, and of course teaming up with a host of unsavory characters to murder Comrade Zhou and grievously wound Comrade Hou.[43] This list of crimes, however, was followed by a note that local opinion held that his punishment should be limited to a term of imprisonment. Again, his lineage members and neighbors didn't want anything too serious to happen to him. After all, he only killed an outsider.

The branch tribunal deciding Big Tiger's fate had two sets of recommendations. Public opinion held that Big Tiger should be sent to prison for a fixed sentence. Township cadres, trained and installed by the Communists, weren't inclined to look kindly at the murder of a political worker. But even they only recommended a life sentence. No one at the local level, it seems, recommended that Big Tiger be put down. The tribunal sided with the masses and handed Big Tiger a four-year prison sentence, further stripping him of his political rights for another five years. According to the judgment of the branch tribunal, Big Tiger shouldn't be killed or locked away forever just because he helped murder a cadre. His fate, however, lay in the hands of the northern cadres running things in Poyang Town. Would they be so forgiving?

Judge Jiang Dispenses Justice at the County Tribunal

Once the case was sent to Poyang Town for review, county security officers took charge of the investigation. Now the interrogation of Big Tiger began in earnest. Back when emperors appointed magistrates to dispense justice from the county yamen, Big Tiger's fate would have been particularly bleak. During the imperial era, torture was an accepted part of the interrogation process. Magistrates assumed that anyone arrested was in fact guilty. If the accused dared to plead innocent, imperial courts used a multiplicity of torture devices to uncover the "truth": a confession of guilt. One nineteenth-century observer described the effects of one of these devices, the dreaded ankle-press, in great detail: "Should the unhappy sufferer be resolute from innocence, or obstinate from guilt, and submit to the consummation of the horrid procedure, his bones are ultimately reduced to a jelly."[44]

Torture had long been outlawed, part of a long and only partly successful push to change negative Western impressions of the Chinese legal system. Harsh punishments, including court-mandated beatings with heavy bamboo rods, had been replaced with hefty fines and lengthy imprisonments.[45] But interrogators still wielded great power and were expected to quickly produce confessions from prisoners. From the stationery used to record the proceeding, we know that Big Tiger's questioner, Officer Shi, worked in the Public Security Bureau's newly established Interrogation Section.[46] Officer Shi and his colleagues had many tools at their disposal. Some interrogators forced prisoners to squat on the floor or sit on low stools, using physical distance to establish their power over the accused. And while historians have uncovered ample evidence of torture in the administration of justice in the People's Republic, security officers typically relied on more subtle techniques to break down prisoners. These included threats of execution and lengthy midnight interrogations, marathon questioning designed to break the spirits of prisoners.[47]

The officers overseeing the county's investigation into Big Tiger now classified him as a farmer and a landlord. From a legal perspective, this made no sense. By definition, landlords didn't engage in agricultural labor. But as Big Tiger's case made its way through the court system of the People's Government, the facts of the case shifted to better fit the party's understanding of what an evil tyrant should look like. There were many of them. In March 1951 the provincial Public Security Bureau reported that in less than half a year over 20,000 evil tyrant landlords had been arrested in Jiangxi.[48]

Officer Shi of the Interrogation Section pressed Big Tiger to reveal exactly what happened to Comrade Zhou back up north in Dayuan Village. Big Tiger continued to emphasize how he had labored in the years before the Communists came to the mountains. But he denied few of the charges levied his way. He held little back. He admitted his ties with the landlord conspirators, as well as his role in the Huang-Li Society. At the behest of the landlords, he now confessed, he led the Fengtian branch of the Huang-Li Society up to Dayuan Village, where they seized Comrade Zhou. Even as he admitted to these crimes, he also tried to lessen his personal guilt. This was his last chance to save himself from the executioner's gun. Big Tiger pointed to one of his henchmen as the true murderer, and he made sure to note that he had, in fact, eventually paid off the injured Comrade Hou with some of the promised grain.[49]

The case finally went to the Poyang County People's Tribunal. The man presiding over this court, Jiang Beiran, was one of the most experienced of the cadres sent south to take control over Poyang's administration. He wasn't from Poyang, but he was no northerner either. Originally from Anhui, a neighboring province where many speak the Gan dialect native to Poyang County, he joined the party back in 1939. Unlike the inexperi-

enced Comrade Zhou he had years of revolutionary practice, conducting
political work for several Communist armies. By the time he arrived in
Poyang he was a true veteran, having survived gunshots to both his ribs
and lungs. Physical disability, however, didn't stop his political rise.[50] Appointed county-chief in September 1949, he played a multiplicity of roles
in Poyang. He was a member of the county party committee, but most of
his administrative posts were in the People's Government. He was headmaster of the Poyang Academy. He supervised the county cooperative. He
ran the People's Court. He led the county Militia Detachment. But for Big
Tiger, most important was Jiang Beiran's role as the presiding judge for
the Poyang County People's Tribunal.[51] Just like magistrates of old, Judge
Jiang held the fates of Poyang's accused criminals in his hands.

The county tribunal, noting that the branch tribunal had sentenced
Big Tiger to four years of jail time, overruled the lower court's initial
verdict. Judge Jiang instead sentenced the former neighborhood-chief to
death. According to this final ruling, authorized in red ink by Judge Jiang's personal seal, Big Tiger was in fact an evil tyrant with a long history
of corruption and bullying the masses. He had attempted to thwart the
redistribution of property by hiding his valuables. Most egregiously, Big
Tiger had organized a reactionary society, allied with enemies of the people, and murdered a People's Liberation Army administrative comrade.
Judge Jiang's verdict, dated March 23, 1951, ruled that Big Tiger was
to be put to death. The tribunal's review board, further explaining the
verdict, noted that the masses had demanded his execution.[52] Big Tiger's
township, of course, had originally requested that he only be sentenced
to jail.

Big Tiger Waits for a Bullet

After sentencing, the wheels of justice continued to move slowly. On
April 25, 1951, one month after sentencing him to death, the county formally requested approval from the higher-ups in the province to execute
Big Tiger as an evil tyrant.[53] Big Tiger now waited. Weeks passed. Then
months passed. As Big Tiger sat in county lockup, the old regime he had
murdered to preserve crumbled. Some of his co-conspirators were already
dead, with at least one taking his own life instead of facing Communist
justice. The Li man who had hosted Comrade Zhou in his house, only to

open his doors to Big Tiger and the assassins, had been executed. Others who had played a role in the murder had been arrested and would share Big Tiger's fate. Warrants were out for the rest of those who had leading roles in the attacks. Some of Big Tiger's minor accomplices were left to the supervision of the masses: placed under surveillance, but not imprisoned.

In February 1952, nearly a year after sentencing the old neighborhood-chief to death, Judge Jiang revisited Big Tiger's case. With approval from above, it was time for him to wrap up the case and end Big Tiger's wait. According to this decision, the final dated document from the county People's Tribunal in the casefile, Judge Jiang once again listed Big Tiger's crimes. This time he added the note that the convicted man had "never engaged in honest work," an odd finding given Big Tiger's long history of farming.[54]

Two months later, his time had finally come. For one last time, Interrogation Section officers asked Big Tiger, evil tyrant, to confess. Questioned on April 26, 1952, Big Tiger answered in ways that showed he had accepted his verdict. Or perhaps security officers made sure his answers fit the narrative they had crafted for his life. Despite the fact that he had been a farmer for most of his life, he now self-identified as a landlord. Before signing his confession, Big Tiger also admitted to an illicit relationship with Ms. Zhao for five years, leading the Huang-Li Society for two years, and serving as a neighborhood-chief prior to liberation.[55] But Big Tiger, perhaps still hoping he could save himself, stopped short of taking full blame for the murder. Admitting to a lesser role in the crimes, he attempted to shift the real responsibility to the wealthy landlords who had masterminded the plot; he was only a "secondary leader."[56] Big Tiger also named two brothers from his own Li lineage as the true bad guys: one had murdered Comrade Zhou while the other attacked Comrade Hou, slashing the man three times in the head and three times in the legs.[57]

Big Tiger never had a chance. As security officers made clear during the investigation, he would have to answer for both his recent crimes and for his past injustices. In the summer of 1949 Big Tiger had led the assassination squad that murdered Comrade Zhou. Everyone knew he did it, but few of his neighbors seemed to care. He remained free until new township leaders had him arrested a year and a half later. A branch tribunal suggested a four-year prison sentence, only to be overruled by the county tribunal. On April 28, 1952, the new regime put Big Tiger down. Convicted as an evil tyrant landlord, he was shot dead in the early afternoon.[58]

The Documents Reach Their Limits

Researching Big Tiger's case, I often found myself confused. This started with Comrade Zhou's mysterious companion, who nearly died that night at the Changshun Pavilion. Who exactly was Comrade Hou? How could he have possibly survived the attack? Why did he never return to seek justice? My students and I also wondered about Ms. Zhao, whose affair with Big Tiger helped seal his fate. Because banditry, counterrevolution, and murder were primarily male fields, she is the only woman mentioned by name in any of the four casefiles profiled in this book. Big Tiger continued the affair for years, but after his own wife died he had no interest in marrying his longtime lover. Big Tiger would later explain that he never remarried out of "concern" for his young son. Refusing remarriage, he instead had his own parents care for his child.[59]

Ms. Zhao's name appears in the documents because of her affair with Big Tiger, but because she never testified, her voice has been lost to history. But we can still find echoes of her agency. She did, after all, take full advantage of the marriage reforms passed during the first years of the People's Republic to divorce her husband. But otherwise, our understanding of Ms. Zhao is filtered through the documents; because she was married during their affair, the relationship was considered illicit by both Nationalist and Communist regimes. According to security officers, Big Tiger had seized and raped her. And yet, why did Big Tiger's confession include the note that he couldn't, or perhaps wouldn't, marry Ms. Zhao? Was his refusal to marry Ms. Zhao because she, rather unfairly given the circumstances, lost considerable status by divorcing her husband? The discussion of a potential marriage between the two, as well as the length of their relationship, serves as a reminder that the legalistic language found in the casefile fails to capture the dynamic role Ms. Zhao must have played in the drama of Big Tiger's downfall.

Reading the casefile, it seems that much is left unsaid, especially as Big Tiger avoided arrest once the Communists came to power. Once again, the limitations of the sources loom large in this story. Things that seemed obvious to security officers and suspects were never formally entered into the record. For example, everyone involved in this case intuitively understood that Big Tiger's allies and extended family were doing everything they could to protect him from justice. Poyang villages were organized by families, which essentially ran local society. A trial such as Big Tiger's was the first crack in breaking clan power. The centrality of the family in these mountains, so essential to every aspect of village life, is never once mentioned in the casefile. Why bother stating the obvious?

Before moving on, three things need emphasis. The first is that we see in this trial just how the party used mass campaigns and the legal system in tandem to bring the power of the state down to village society. Much to their credit, the Communists paid attention to law and the will of the masses to legitimize their actions. The party didn't send in the People's Liberation Army to execute Big Tiger on the spot. He was arrested, investigated, and tried by a court of law. As part of that trial, moreover, the party carefully considered public opinion. Because his neighbors wanted him alive, the branch tribunal initially gave him a fixed prison term, despite the fact that the township government recommended a life sentence. The attention the party lavished on rural society goes a long way to explain why so many farmers welcomed the People's Government. Here, at long last, was a state that seemed to value rural citizens.

This included a commitment to putting previously disadvantaged villagers into leadership positions. This leads to a second point of emphasis: the party's first rural campaigns demolished the old elite. Some went on their own accord. Readers may have noted that this casefile made repeated references to runaway landlords, wealthy men who gathered what they could and hit the road before the Communists came calling. This is one of the many sad ironics to emerge from the first years of the People's Republic. The wealthiest individuals, who had benefited the most from the old order, were long gone by the time the Communists and their legal system showed up. That left men like Big Tiger to stand trial for not only their own crimes, but the crimes of the old regime they once served. He was only one of 1,396 Poyang men charged as evil tyrant landlords, about one for every three neighborhoods in the county.[60] Once these small-fry, the hamlet-chiefs and neighborhood-chiefs of old, were dealt with, the old ties between state power and villages were no more. In their place rose a new leadership core, including the chair of the peasant association.

At the same time, however, we see that the party's commitment to truth and the masses had real limits with real consequences. And that brings us to the third point: the weaponized words of the revolution became especially dangerous as they became disconnected from the reality of the rural scene. As Big Tiger worked his way through the court system, officers steadily adjusted his class status to better fit their understandings of what a counterrevolutionary looked like.[61] No longer a laboring peasant, Big Tiger ended up branded as a landlord. A farmer his entire life, he was convicted of living off the labor of the exploited masses. Just as had been the case when Old Six and Old Seven died as Nationalist loyalists, it was the label and not the reality that mattered. And as for Big Tiger's fate, the suggestions of the masses were in the end just that, suggestions. The final judgment lay with the county government, where cadres didn't look kindly at the murder of one of their own. As we will see in casefile 3, this included murders that occurred decades before the establishment of the People's Republic.

CASEFILE 3
THE CASE OF THE
BODHISATTVA SOCIETY

Cast of Characters (in order of appearance)

Runaway Xu: Landlord turned undercover agent
Comrade Cheng: Cheng Yangshan, martyred in 1930
Kuang Rong'en: Betrayed Comrade Cheng in 1930
Landlord Hua: Kuang family member, escaped from jail
Middle Peasant Mai: Kuang family member, holder of his village
   bodhisattva statue
Zhu Guo: Landlord, escaped from jail
Landlord Zhao: Rumored to be alive after dying during the jailbreak
Zhu Shuyi: Zhu Guo's son and Public Security Bureau employee
Daoist Zou: Landlord, hiding out in Lushan Village
Kuang Number Four: Peasant, member of the Bodhisattva Society

A Landlord Provides a Thread

He reached the end of his rope in the summer of 1951, over two years
after the Communists officially liberated Poyang. Originally from the
mountainous north, not far from where Golden Cao and his bandit gang
once roamed, Runaway Xu had no place else to run. He had fled from
land reform, the campaign that brought the revolution down to each and

every village governed by the People's Republic. Land reform included the distribution of class labels, a process that divided peasants, the friends of the revolution, from landlords, who were assumed to long for the return of the Nationalists. Like many Poyang men given the dreaded landlord class label, Runaway Xu chose to flee from home rather than face the ritualized humiliation and violence that accompanied land reform.[1] In Jiangxi work team cadres initially wavered between conducting "peaceful" land reform, free of violence, and letting poor villagers beat and terrorize landlords. Some cadres, not knowing how much wealth landlords might have stashed away, used torture to get everything they could from their victims. With the party increasingly stressing the pitfalls of peaceful land reform, violence became widespread. Wealthy farmers started to panic. Many landlords decided that staying put and waiting for rural revolution was a death wish. In one county more than 3,000 landlords fled.[2]

Runaway Xu was far from alone in making the decision to escape his village before land reform brought New China to his doorstep. He may have hoped to make his way south to Hong Kong, but he couldn't even get out of Poyang. And now he was alone, with nowhere else to go. Defeated, he turned himself in to the new order. That meant questioning from officers in the Political Defense Section. The Section was new, formed by the county Public Security Bureau in that same year of 1951, just a few months after widespread paranoia over the threat of counterrevolution had launched a nationwide campaign to root out dissent.[3] These officers, in charge of investigating crimes, interrogating suspects, and uncovering counterrevolution, were about to have the case of their young careers.

Meeting with security officers in the Political Defense Section, the fugitive landlord found redemption. Runaway Xu offered up what the officers would later call a "thread": a lead on two notorious criminals, both landlords from the Old County Crossing area. Security officers knew that corner of the countryside much better as the People's Government's newly created Fourth District. These two landlords, arrested by their district government during land reform, had conducted a brazen jailbreak and disappeared into the countryside. Their daring act had created a ripple effect in surrounding villages. News of their escape fueled rumors linking their movements to the return of the old Nationalist regime. One wild rumor even claimed that a third landlord, killed during the jailbreak, had returned from the dead to terrorize the Communists.

The officers taking Runaway Xu's statement must have been familiar with the case of the escaped criminal landlords. There was, after all, an ongoing investigation into the duo's whereabouts. They had been underground for over four months by the time Runaway Xu showed up. Were they still even in Poyang? A troubling case made even more disturbing by the wild rumors of an undead landlord roaming the mountains. But this case must have been particularly special for the men of the county Public Security Bureau. One of these two criminal landlords, a man they had been trying in vain to track down, was the father of one of their agency colleagues.

An Old Revolutionary Gets Martyred

Runaway Xu gave the Political Defense officers a thread that would link the two escapees to a murder long past. And not just any murder, but the 1930 execution of Comrade Cheng Yangshan. Even in these first days of the People's Republic, Comrade Cheng was already considered an "old revolutionary." Exactly what happened to the old revolutionary is unclear. The casefile in question contains almost nothing on Comrade Cheng, except a stray note that his hometown was now part of the newly created First District. Luckily, Poyang historians have lavished much attention on martyrs such as Comrade Cheng. Born in 1896, he had a short but eventful career as a Communist organizer. He joined the party in the spring of 1930 during a hightide of rural activism. Local Communists, under orders to jumpstart the revolution in the countryside, went all out to organize poor villagers. The party's county branch promoted peasant uprisings in support of newly formed governments at the district and township levels. The Red Tenth Army even seized Poyang Town. In retaliation the Nationalists mobilized a massive force, backed by gunboats sailing on Lake Poyang.[4] Chiang Kai-shek failed to annihilate the Communists once and for all, but forces led by local Nationalists hunted down rural revolutionaries, creating no shortage of martyrs. One of them was Comrade Cheng.

The documents in the casefile are unconcerned with the circumstances of Comrade Cheng's martyrdom. But according to Poyang's official history, Comrade Cheng had been an able organizer, mobilizing farmers in dozens of villages to support the Communists and punish hated rural bosses. After

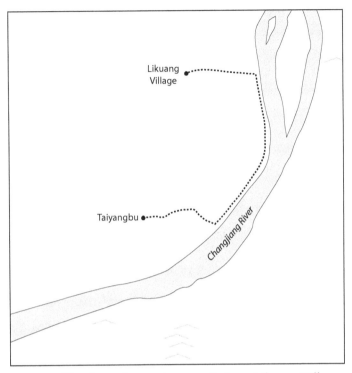

Map 12. The short ninety-minute walk from Likuang Village to Taiyangbu, where Comrade Cheng was arrested.

the Red Tenth Army was pushed out of Poyang, Comrade Cheng stayed behind to keep the revolution alive. Then, on the afternoon of December 13, he was betrayed by a man named Kuang Rong'en. Comrade Cheng was captured alive at Taiyangbu, just down river from Likuang Village, where Kuang was a leading citizen, and dragged down to Poyang Town. The Nationalists executed Comrade Cheng the very next day.[5]

Not long after the Communists liberated Poyang, the dead man's brother journeyed to Likuang Village. [6] With the new regime coalescing, he must have known that the time had come to seek justice. Kuang Rong'en, the man who betrayed his brother, was long gone. But the man's family was still in Likuang Village, and he could hold them accountable for getting his brother martyred. Demanding a payoff in return for a life lost almost two decades earlier, this outsider held the fate of the Kuang

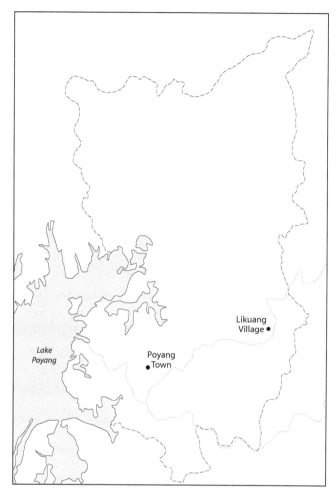

Map 13. Likuang Village, home to the Bodhisattva
Society.

family in his hands. As he made clear, if his demands were not met, he
would turn to the People's Government for justice.[7]

Two Kuangs Form the Bodhisattva Society

The martyr's brother arrived in Likuang Village at a time of transition.
Tellingly, the village took half of its name from its most powerful lineage:
the Kuangs. The Likuang Village order was led by Hua and Mai, two
Kuang men in different economic situations. According to the Commu-

nists, Hua was a landlord, while Mai was a middle peasant. This would make the first a class enemy, the second a potential ally. But both men were members of the Nationalist Party and graduates of Poyang Academy, the closest thing to a modern school in Poyang. Hua had graduated from a teaching college before serving in multiple positions for the old regime at the township and county levels. Mai was a farmer with a surprising military background. According to a later report, after graduating from Poyang Academy he had gone on to study at Whampoa Military Academy, the famous training center established by the Nationalists during their initial alliance with the Communists. In the rhetoric of New China this made him a *fake* military officer.[8]

One a landlord and the other a farmer, Hua and Mai were united in their control over their village even as they occupied different roles in the rural economy. But times were changing. Faced with this demand for a payoff to compensate the Cheng family for the life of their martyred relative, the two men quickly moved to keep their secrets safe from outsiders. Villagers in Poyang often came together to settle disputes and deal with outside threats. Some formed village compacts, especially smaller communities with powerful clans. Typically included alongside genealogical records, these compacts regulated local society, detailing ideal behavior for villagers. Compacts also included instructions for protecting local forests, safeguarding crops from theft, and fighting bandits.[9] What happened in Likuang Village, however, was much more than a reading of the village compact. Calling a meeting at Middle Peasant Mai's house, the Kuang clan gathered dozens of village "bosses" together to discuss how they could compensate the outsider and keep their secrets hidden away from the Communists. That very night they swore a sacred oath of loyalty to each other. Sworn oaths among men, modeled after the fabled "Peach Tree Oath" taken by the heroes of the epic novel *The Romance of the Three Kingdoms*, were not to be taken lightly.

The men of the village took their oaths in front of a small statue, the centerpiece for local religious practice. Out of concern for its safety, it had just recently been moved from its original public location into Middle Peasant Mai's house. This statue would play an outsized role in the drama to come. The officers investigating the case, dismissive of religion as mere superstition, paid little attention to the statue. But this object of worship held great power, venerated by villagers when they prayed for fortune and good health. All that we really know about the diminutive statue is that Likuang villagers called it a *bodhisattva*. In Buddhism bodhisattvas are enlightened beings who dedicate themselves to helping others. Locally in Poyang, "bodhisattva" was used as a catch-all term for the gods that villagers turned to in times of need.[10] Security officers, however, made sure to call it a *fake* bodhisattva.

In front of their bodhisattva, the villagers drank rooster blood mixed with wine. They vowed to protect their homes, cultivate their hearts, accumulate merit, and do good deeds to ensure their next lives. These tales of ritualistically drinking rooster blood, found in the documents created by security officers investigating this case, tied the villagers to some of the most important traditions of secret societies. Many secret society rituals culminated in the drinking of wine mixed with rooster blood. During initiation rituals for new members of the Gowned Brothers, an underground organization on the Chengdu plain, society elders mixed blood from a freshly killed rooster with wine. New members drank the blood wine as part of their oath-taking ceremony.[11] The sacrifice of a rooster had long been a potent symbol used in Daoist and later Buddhist rituals, and was eventually adopted by secret societies.

The use of Buddhist rituals by secret societies, as well as the deep reverence for the bodhisattva statue, should be expected. Buddhist beliefs and practices permeated the Poyang countryside. Local Buddhist practice was primarily lay in nature: in 1949 the county only had forty or so nuns and monks. But every village had believers, who congregated at the hundreds of temples scattered throughout the countryside. Most of these religious sites featured a statue or image of a Buddhist figure, such as Guanyin or an Arhat. Many were destroyed during Japanese invasion. But Likuang, like nearly all Poyang villages, still had its bodhisattva.

Deeply religious villagers believed the bodhisattva statue to possess great power. There was a long history of religious practices built around Buddhist beliefs in Poyang, many of which are decidedly fantastical. Hong Mai, perhaps Poyang's most famous scholar, included some local tales of the supernatural in his classic *Record of Hearsay*. Buddhist mediums were said to recite spells that allowed them to enter boiling water and fire. These mediums gave Hong's own brother instructions to cure diseases through Buddhist incantations, invoking the name of Nagarjuna, an ancient Buddhist philosopher, to cure blisters.[12] Such fantastic tales aside, Poyang families turned to Buddhism largely due to their faith in bodhisattvas, enlightened beings who promised to rescue the faithful in their times of need, including moments of great peril.[13] In a world with almost no healthcare and high child mortality rates, this promise of hope gave these diminutive Buddhist statues considerable power in Poyang villages.

As the holder of the bodhisattva, Middle Peasant Mai took the lead in cementing village unity to protect the secrets of the Kuang clan, telling his rooster blood brothers to spread the word that everyone should go all out to protect them, lest they suffer a calamity themselves. If they had any questions they could come ask the bodhisattva, conveniently located in his house, for answers. This gave him and Landlord Hua considerable sway over their highly religious neighbors. The men, forming what security officers later called the "Bodhisattva Society," seemed to have figured out a way to buy the silence of Comrade Cheng's family: the dead man's brother was among those at the secretive meeting. Unfortunately, that did nothing to solve their much larger problem. They could buy off a family, but not the People's Republic.

Land Reform Reveals a Powerful State

Poyang villagers first saw the power of the Communists flow from the barrels of the guns of the People's Liberation Army, which had wielded murderous firepower on the mountains in the northern part of the county. Grain requisitions, despite the occasional murder of cadres, had also flexed the strength of the new regime. But it was land reform that truly cemented Communist power in the countryside. These campaigns of rural revolution brought state power to the grassroots in a manner unimaginable in earlier regimes.

During land reform, the Communist Party promoted a standardized script to remake rural societies from the bottom up. Work teams arrived in villages, sought out the poorest farmers, and mobilized activists to confront, humiliate, and attack their wealthy neighbors. It was a script perfected in a novel penned by Ding Ling, who had observed land reform firsthand at the start of the Civil War. Alongside her during those days was her husband, Chen Ming, a Poyang native. Chen, who would one day write in glowing terms of his early life near the vast waters of Lake Poyang, worked with Ding Ling as she fashioned their real-life experiences into narrative form. In a very real sense, the campaigns of rural revolution that came to Poyang had been influenced by one of their own.

The campaigns began with "test point" land reform in June 1950. This was a limited and focused campaign, designed above all to give experience to work team members. Land reform work teams, composed of soldiers and cadres from the top ranks of the new county government, began the process of rural revolution in Qingzhu Township in the newly created Eighth District, headquartered in Forty Mile Street. Soon work teams composed of nearly 500 cadres, soldiers, activists, and intellectuals brought land reform to every village in the district. Hundreds more would join work teams as rural revolution spread throughout Poyang. By the time the campaigns ended in the early spring of 1951, party-organized work teams, working with newly established peasant associations, had labeled nearly 5,000 landlord households.[14] These families would lose some of their property as it was redistributed to their neighbors; because many resisted these changes, with land reform came criminal charges.

Work Teams Discover Criminals

The new Poyang government utilized land reform as a moment to expand judicial and state power out from Poyang Town and into the countryside. This necessitated courts and prisons to deal with any locals who dared to push back against the People's Government. As readers will recall from Big Tiger's case, the county established a People's Tribunal and eight branch tribunals to handle these cases. After dealing with evil tyrants such as Big Tiger, the tribunals turned to land reform cases. During the first stage of land reform in Poyang, the new regime arrested 1,587 people, or about one criminal landlord for every three neighborhoods in the county. Among them, 322 were executed. Uncovering past crimes was an essential part of the land reform process. Work teams, trained to assume the countryside remained under the control of class enemies, searched for those who had mistreated their neighbors during the old regime. Villagers could also report past abuses to a visiting work team or directly to township or district governments. Once a work team or local government filed a formal accusation, the People's Tribunal had the authority to arrest, interrogate, and prosecute suspected criminals.[15]

We know some of Poyang's criminal landlords. Lian Hanzhang, a member of the Nationalist Party branded as a criminal landlord, was sentenced to three years in prison for concealing his property and refusing to hand over grain to the new order. A similar sentence was given to Wu Zhantai, a landlord who attempted to bribe a cadre into improving his class status. Even landlords attempting to submit to the new order might find themselves arrested as criminals. Over in the Ninth District, the landlord Huang Huangle had prospered in the old regime. Laboring for twenty years, Huang and his brother had accumulated enough capital to lend money, using the profits from high-interest loans to invest in land. He lost his house in land reform, as well as his entire storage of grain. When the work team demanded more grain to pay off past exploitation, he exploded in anger: "Again demanding so much grain from me, my family has nothing left to eat, I won't hand anything over, go ahead and lock me up, I have nothing left to give." The work team called his bluff and took him into custody. But because the masses were a critical part of the reporting process, tribunals sometimes took it easy on well-liked or respected villagers. Huang, known locally as a hard worker, was given a reduced sentence after his neighbors petitioned for his release.[16]

A Secret Is Revealed and Two Landlords Get Arrested

These criminal landlords, typically wealthy men who broke the law while resisting confiscations, were mostly guilty of economic crimes. Landlord Hua, on the other hand, shared much more in common with those the party labeled evil tyrants. Big Tiger, for example, had led an assassination squad to murder a cadre. The connection between Comrade Cheng's martyrdom in 1930 and later events is unclear, but all available evidence suggests that Landlord Hua had led the way in covering up the betrayal of an old revolutionary. Exactly how the work team linked the crime to Landlord Hua will forever remain a mystery. The casefile in question contains no clue as to what exactly happened in Likuang Village during land reform.

Here's what can be said about Landlord Hua, who like Big Tiger was charged as an evil tyrant landlord. He was of middling importance in Poyang. After finishing his studies at Poyang Academy, Hua had graduated from a teacher-training school in 1932. He then taught for three years before moving into government work. He held several positions for the Nationalists, including posts in education and military affairs, before returning home in 1941 to run a small business.

On November 19, 1950, almost certainly due to his role in covering up the martyrdom of the old revolutionary Comrade Cheng, the People's Government arrested Landlord Hua. What security officers would later call the Bodhisattva Society, however tight-knit, probably had no chance against the work team stationed in Likuang Village. These teams, while composed entirely of outsiders, had training in seeking out past injustices far smaller than the murder of an old revolutionary. Teams "squatted on a point," staying in villages for extended periods of time to examine social and economic conditions. Practicing the "three togethers" they lived, ate, and worked with villagers to mobilize the poorest among them to embrace the Communists and their revolution.[17] It was only a matter of time before the team developed local activists and discovered Landlord Hua's crime. Arrested by the new regime, Landlord Hua sat in a local detention center awaiting trial. There he met Zhu Guo. The two men's fates quickly became intwined.

The two had much in common. Both were Nationalist Party members who had served the old regime in several posts, only to now find themselves detained by the People's Government. But Zhu Guo, whose original crime goes entirely unmentioned in the casefile, had a particularly messy family situation: his son, Zhu Shuyi, was a People's Government bureaucrat, posted in the Public Security Bureau. Zhu Shuyi had originally signed up to serve the Nationalist regime in Poyang Town, only to find himself working for the Communists when the newly arrived cadres took over the Public Security Bureau and its employees. He was transferred in late 1949 to the bureau's Interrogation Section to handle administrative work. Shortly after his transfer, provincial party leaders, concerned with the large number of government offices staffed with holdovers from the Nationalist era, asked all work units to conduct an internal cleansing. All employees, down to cleaning staff and drivers, were to be investigated.[18]

Any sort of internal cleansing was bound to cause problems for Zhu Shuyi. He could have claimed illness or otherwise found an excuse to resign. But he stayed on with the county Public Security Bureau and seems to have passed his review without incident. Then his father was arrested as a criminal landlord. On February 22, 1951, his father made his life even more difficult by joining Landlord Hua's jailbreak. This was a serious offense against the new regime. Prison guards had the authority to shoot escapees dead.[19] Indeed, during the jailbreak a third escapee, Landlord Zhao of Wuchang Village, was caught and beaten to death by angry militiamen.[20] Before his father's arrest, Zhu Shuyi was said to be quite energetic and active in his work. Later his colleagues in the Public Security Bureau would say that in his heart he was very uneasy. And he told anyone who would listen that his father wasn't to blame. Secretly, his colleagues would come to believe, he found ways to contact his father and help hide him from the new regime.

Two Landlords Go on the Run, One Landlord Returns from Hell

After their escape from the detention center, the two men first fled to Luyuan Village, where Landlord Hua's mother-in-law lived. Later they made their way to Zhu Guo's old house, where they dug out a basement cellar. They kept moving, switching residences several times to evade the Communists. At one point they lived in a secret room, concealed behind a fake wall. They separated for a time: Zhu Guo returned home to Zhujia Village, living in a large house on the water. During this visit home, some fishermen from Jiazhou Village, upriver from Zhujia, saw him standing on the shore at night. Spotted, the landlord went back on the run. Local peasants helped him hide out and make his way to Likuang Village.[21] As they reasoned, the Likuang Village bodhisattva had predicted the return of the Nationalists. And in any case, didn't Zhu Guo's son work in the powerful Public Security Bureau? Family bonds were the surest thing in the countryside, more valuable than banknotes. Protecting the father was a smart way to win the favor of the son.

Both men eventually made their way to Likuang Village. Landlord Hua's hometown must have seemed the best place to hide out. Even here in relative safety, they kept moving, shuffling between the homes of various members of the Kuang clan, who could all be trusted to keep their secrets. This network of closely related families, security officers alleged, was in fact the counterrevolutionary Bodhisattva Society. According to the reports left behind by officers, the two fugitive landlords relied on the superstitious nature of Likuang villagers to conceal their evil deeds and slander the Communists. They utilized the county's rivers and lakes to quickly move from place to place and expand their reach. In the name of their village bodhisattva statue, they declared the redistribution of land unjust. Using "lies to intimidate the masses," they boldly claimed that Landlord Zhao, their fellow escapee, was still among the living.[22] According to the legend that was now making the rounds, Landlord Zhao had been beaten to death during the jailbreak and sent back home, where he made a miraculous recovery. He had met with Yama, the Buddhist King of Hell, and come back to life with a mission.

Landlord Zhao's fantastic journey to hell and back would have made perfect sense to Poyang villagers. The popular understanding of Yama, like so many other aspects of Buddhism, underwent drastic changes as the religion made its way east from the Indian subcontinent. In India, Buddhists believed that the laws of karma operated automatically as the dead were reborn into their next lives. As the lord of the underworld, Yama had no real power and was little more than an ineffectual bureaucrat. As Buddhism came to East Asia, however, conceptions of the afterlife shifted to reflect local beliefs. Reincarnation was replaced by eternal happiness in the Pure Land or endless punishments in hell. And in a telling reflection of the powers held by Chinese officials from the Lord of Po to the new county-chief Jiang Beiran, Yama was granted great authority to decide the fates of the dead.[23]

Yama ordered Landlord Zhao to return to the world of the living, or at least that was what villagers were saying. It wasn't his time to die. And besides, he had great things to accomplish. His return from the dead was linked with the fates of the two landlords who had survived the jailbreak, as well as a promised return of the Nationalists to Poyang. The two men should thus not be punished for their crimes. The runaways were said to have even composed a poem to congratulate Landlord Zhao on his rebirth from Buddhist hell: "Riches and honor are in Heaven, Heaven determines wealth, health is precious, life and death are in accordance with fate, if one is not fated to die, one will come back to life."[24] Landlord Zhao seemed to be not only alive, but actively resisting the new Communist regime; members of the Bodhisattva Society claimed that the resurrected landlord had been setting fires in nearby mountains.[25]

Back in Likuang Village, the escaped landlords had to keep hidden away. Luckily Kuang Mai, labeled a peasant during land reform, could help. Not long ago, Middle Peasant Mai and Landlord Hua had rallied their relatives and other allies to pay off Comrade Cheng's family. Now they gathered their neighbors once more to keep their whereabouts hidden from the Communists. Meeting at Middle Peasant Mai's house, they brought the Bodhisattva Society back together to face a new challenge. This second meeting, consisting of a couple dozen locals, was led by Middle Peasant Mai and the two escaped landlords. Many of those present belonged to what the Communist called the "peasant masses," the humble farmers who should have embraced the revolution. According to one report, the peasant association's entire leadership core was in attendance.[26] Once again, they drank wine mixed with rooster blood and swore oaths in front of the village's revered bodhisattva statue, vowing to protect the two fugitive landlords from discovery.

Daoist Zou Divines the Future, Landlords Form a Shrimp Opera Troupe

Poyang security officers later made sure to delegitimize this group as a *fake* peasant association, as opposed to a real peasant association that brought state power down to the village level. According to officers, Bodhisattva Society members were determined to spare no effort in service of the two criminals and would act as their eyes and ears, reporting on what the authorities knew about their whereabouts. This would allow the fugitive landlords to plan how to deal with the government and lower the political consciousness of the masses, so that they might continue to hide out, safe from the authorities until they could get out of Poyang for good.[27] According to one later accounting, the secret society had 140 members, including 12 militiamen.

Officers linked their conspiracy to other Poyang residents. Some lived nearby, like the fugitive landlord Daoist Zou, who was hiding out in Lushan Village, just across the river from Likuang. Daoist Zou, claiming an immortal spirit had taught him a method for divining the future, predicted the death of Mao Zedong and the return of Chiang Kai-shek and the Nationalists. Superstitious villagers, believing the Communists were sure to fall from power, let him hide out in Lushan. Another Bodhisattva Society rumor claimed that in Shanghai people were saying that "America is going to drop an atomic bomb, and it will decimate the People's Liberation Army."[28]

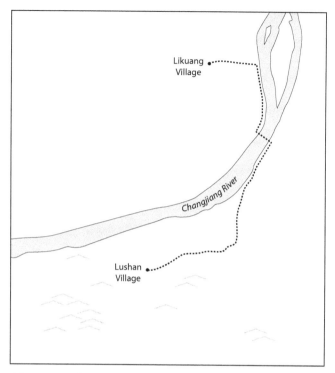

Map 14. A short ninety-minute journey from Likuang to Lushan Village.

Poyang officers also found links between the Bodhisattva Society and the powerful Zhang family, located in the county's First District, based in White Deer Wharf. The Zhangs were also helping one of their own to hide out from the Communists, although much of their supposed counter-revolutionary activities seem to have been out in the open. Most notably, the Zhang clan organized a small militia of twenty to thirty men, as well as an opera troupe that the Communists accused of spreading counter-revolutionary messages.

The Communists viewed opera, and the performing arts in general, as a cultural weapon. This was a weapon that had to be wielded by the party. The party had already intervened in the local cultural scene, organizing schools to stage operas created up north during the long struggle against Japan. In preparation for land reform, students from Poyang Academy, where Landlord Hua had once attended school, staged a trio of red classics. *The White-Haired Girl* told the story of a sexually abused

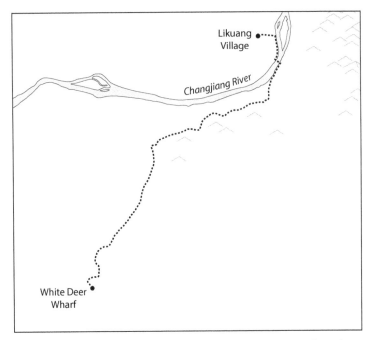

Map 15. The Zhang clan hailed from the First District, based in White Deer Wharf, a five-hour hike from Likuang Village.

poor peasant girl who gained revenge on her tormentors when her village was liberated by the Communists. *Liu Hulan* dramatized the real-life story of a peasant girl who defiantly chose martyrdom rather than betray the revolution. And *Brother and Sister Open Wasteland* celebrated rural laborers.[29]

As the Communists discovered during their early experiments with dramatic forms of propaganda, rural audiences expressed a deep preference for their local operatic traditions. Poyang was no different. Chen Ming, who had accompanied his wife Ding Ling as she penned a highly influential account of land reform, had attended school in Poyang Town. He had fond memories of eating tasty bowls of seafood noodles and watching modern plays featuring impassioned speeches by politically minded students.[30] In the countryside, however, villagers flocked to see Rao River Opera. These operas had dominated the local cultural scene since the late imperial era, and many opera troupes traveled the countryside staging their shows. The market town of Jiantian Street, for example, built an opera stage in 1874 and eventually hosted a dozen or so opera troupes. Most of these were simple outfits, known locally as Crown Prince troupes.

According to security officers, the landlords of the powerful Zhang clan had organized their own Crown Prince opera troupe to confuse and depress the spirits of the masses. But these kinds of troupes were in fact very common in the countryside. Because these were essentially amateur outfits with very little training and even less equipment, Crown Prince troupes were often derided as "shrimp" troupes. Operating on a yearly cycle, shrimp troupes would begin studying an opera in the spring, have dress rehearsal during Dragon Boat Festival, debut a formal performance at Mid-Autumn Festival, and perform in nearby towns and villages for a fee during the New Year celebrations.[31]

The Communists, on the lookout for any threat to the new regime, didn't take kindly to unauthorized drama troupes. Their own revolutionary operas depicted the official view of the countryside. Audiences took in shows portraying honest peasants squaring off against reactionary landlords. Who knew what counterrevolutionary dramas a landlord-controlled shrimp troupe might stage? Security officers quickly interpreted the Zhang family's formation of an opera troupe as a reactionary plot to trick the masses. They also believed that the fugitive landlord families had established an underground network to keep each other safe. As they saw things, the Zhang and Kuang families knew each other's secrets and did their best to help each other keep these secrets hidden from the Communists. If the Kuang family's secrets were discovered, they could find shelter with the Zhang family, and vice versa.

A Landlord Secret Agent Goes Undercover

Runaway Xu, himself a refugee landlord and graduate of Poyang Academy, had been privy to some of these secrets. So when he reached the end of his rope in the summer of 1951 he spilled his guts, telling Political Defense Section officers everything he knew about the jailbreak and its aftermath. His confession almost certainly saved his life. He was a landlord on the run, but his surrender and confession made him a progressive element, worthy of reeducation instead of execution. But how to proceed? According to their new informant, the two escaped landlords had organized a network of villagers, nearly all of them close relatives, to help keep them hidden from probing eyes. Officers, trained to see counterrevolution everywhere, quickly identified this as a reactionary secret society. Such a target represented a formidable challenge, but as the security officers prepared their investigation they had a secret weapon: Runaway Xu. He knew firsthand the types of schemes the two escapees were using to stay undetected, so why not use him to flush the men out of hiding? As the officers later noted, the first step was providing the runaway with an "ideological education."

How, exactly, did security officers provide Runaway Xu with an ideological education? Here their reports are silent. But the creation of revolutionary colleges and political training classes, the dispatching of the educated elite to the countryside in work teams, and round after round of thought reform provide clues. Many Chinese citizens attended short-term training courses, learning about the importance of labor and how to understand Marxist historical development. Courses, including lessons on the Chinese revolution and the necessity of class struggle, were followed by pointed group discussion and self-criticism.[32] By breaking down these students before rebuilding them, the party offered a chance for redemption.

The casefile in question offers no evidence that Runaway Xu ever studied Marxist theory under the tutelage of the Political Defense Section. Perhaps a few strong words on class enemies sufficed to educate him on the errors of his ways. What is clear is this: Runaway Xu's ideological education indeed hinged on an offer of redemption. Poyang security officers made it clear that only by bringing the fugitive landlords to justice could he save his own life. They would use a thief to catch a thief or, as one officer poetically phrased it, "use poison to fight poison."[33] The fled landlord took the hint, asking to help atone for his crimes and save his life. He would become an undercover agent, reassuming his role as a landlord on the run, to help locate the two wanted men.

To be sure, cultivating a secret agent, what officers called an "insider," was almost unheard of in the countryside.[34] The Public Security Bureau did recruit secret agents to infiltrate suspect groups, but almost always in cities, not rural places like sleepy Poyang Town. During the early years of the People's Republic, some senior public security officers had promoted recruiting secret agents in the countryside, but most were decidedly skeptical about villagers serving as insiders. They also doubted that the officers working at a rural Public Security Bureau such as the one in Poyang were up to the challenge of overseeing undercover cases. Not long after the founding of New China, bureau leadership officially discouraged the idea of recruiting agents in the countryside.[35]

These concerns were far removed from the minds of the officers in Poyang Town. As they would prove once the matter was concluded, they didn't lack confidence in their talents. Getting approval from their superiors in the Political Defense Section, the security officers sent Runaway Xu to investigate the situation in Likuang Village and ascertain exactly where the fugitive landlords were hiding.[36] Everything was to be done in secret and, as luck would have it, the county Public Security Bureau oversaw a farm not far from Likuang Village. The farm, which helped feed security officers throughout the county, was a large one with rice paddies, dry land crops, and almost 800 pear trees.[37]

Two security officers were dispatched to the farm to coordinate with Runaway Xu's undercover agent work and directly report back to their agency colleagues as the investigation progressed. County bureau leaders granted them flexibility while they were in the field. The two fugitive landlords had to be caught.

Venturing to Likuang Village, Runaway Xu easily passed himself off as a refugee landlord, on the run from the Communists and land reform. He understood the fear that came with the landlord class label, and the desperation that drove a landlord to flee from home with nowhere to run. In this regard he was a natural. But his sudden appearance and overzealous probing quickly aroused suspicion. Likuang villagers, after all, were attempting to protect their own fugitives. Who exactly was this guy? Was he part of the ongoing hunt for the fled landlords? Might he be an undercover agent? Suspicious of his motives, villagers urged him to just go away.

Runaway Xu did, but only to report to his handlers back at the agency's farm. Under their careful instruction, he returned to Likuang Village and begged Kuang Number Four, one of the peasants protecting the fled landlords, for shelter. Runaway Xu was getting better at acting, bowing respectfully with clasped hands until the peasant, far too trusting of this outsider, relented. Farming with Kuang Number Four during the day, he slept at the peasant's house at night. Every three days he carefully found

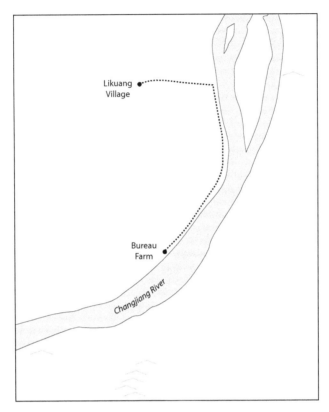

Map 16. The short half-hour walk from the Bureau Farm
to Likuang Village.

the time to return and update the security officers assigned to the bureau's
farm. This way he was able to get room and board while he snooped
around the village and did his best to charm Kuang Number Four. According to his handlers, Runaway Xu uncovered how the Bodhisattva
Society hid weapons, used superstition to numb the masses, and helped
shield the two landlords from view as they went back and forth between
their hiding places.

Kuang Number Four Spills the Beans

Runaway Xu revealed how the two fugitives would lay low during the
day and move from house to house at night. Because his own questioning
continued to arouse suspicion, the two security officers stationed at the

bureau's farm helped with the investigation, hiding out at night around the outskirts of Likuang Village in hopes of spying any movement. Sneaking through fields and eavesdropping on suspects, they discovered valuable intel on where the criminals were going and who was helping them avoid detection. More than anything, their stakeout confirmed the reports they had been getting from their informant. They could trust their insider.

Kuang Number Four, having naively taken pity on the undercover agent, eventually spilled the beans. Middle Peasant Mai and the two fugitive landlords were planning on traveling to Hong Kong. The rivers surrounding Lake Poyang were jammed with commercial traffic, offering plenty of opportunities for escape. Kuang Number Four naively urged his new friend to get a travel certificate so that he could escape New China as well. After Runaway Xu reported all this back to his handlers, they showed just how much they trusted him, giving him his own travel certificate so he could learn more about the men's plans. Soon their insider relayed back that the fugitives, rightfully getting nervous, were just about ready to make their move. Time was short, so without asking for permission from upper-level leadership, they had a quick discussion with the head of the Political Defense Section. Then they made their move. It was time to bring the case to a close.

Runaway Xu had reported that the men had prepared a small arsenal of knives, spears, and other weapons in preparation of their journey. The fugitives were naturally worried about security officers, which made the investigation particularly difficult. But their hard work paid off. On August 9, 1951, the officers stationed at the bureau farm mobilized all available farmhands and set off to Likuang Village. Coordinating with the local government, which had mobilized about a dozen militiamen, they captured all three criminals. They also unearthed a homemade cannon, two bolt-action rifles, two homemade rifles, five broadswords, a pair of double knives, one knife, five spears, and an iron rod. According to the security officers who cracked the case, the fugitive landlords, after laying low for nearly half of a year, had planned one last attack before they fled to Hong Kong.[38]

Only the Audacious: Talented Security Officers Congratulate Themselves

The exact fate of the three criminals remains a mystery. No doubt they were punished severely. In addition to their original crimes, that jail-break was a serious offense. Except for attacking a guard, it was the most heinous prison crime imaginable.[39] There is a very good chance that all three were executed for their actions. They had, after all, broken the law both before and after the arrival of the Communists. But the rank-and-file members of the Bodhisattva Society largely avoided punishment. The county Public Security Bureau made sure to draw a distinction between counterrevolutionaries and good but momentarily confused citizens. Some of the wealthier villagers drawn into the orbit of the Bodhisattva Society were given the rare label of "progressive landlord." This included Daoist Zou, who was said to have been tricked into spreading rumors concerning the return of Chiang Kai-shek and the Nationalists.[40]

Commenting on the successful close of the case, the Public Security Bureau focused on the powers of counterrevolution in Poyang. According to officers, the case of the Bodhisattva Society proved that the crimes of evil tyrant landlords knew no bounds, and that among the masses there were many who were woefully confused about the lines between friends and foes. This represented a grave threat to the revolution. Luckily, the case had proven the mettle of the "audacious and talented" security officers.[41]

Wrapping up the case, security officers reinvestigated the whereabouts of Landlord Zhao, the escapee who was said to have returned to life after meeting the King of Hell. Determined to prove that he had in fact been killed by overzealous militiamen, officers traveled to Landlord Zhao's home village. There they dug up his grave for inspection, unearthing his rotten corpse. This was in some ways a shocking act. In Poyang digging up the grave of someone's ancestor was regarded as a particularly scandalous offense.[42] Here at last, however, was definitive proof that the landlord had in fact died during the jailbreak.

Zhu Shuyi, under investigation for helping his father evade his colleagues in the Public Security Bureau, was asked to consider why he took pity on his father and helped him evade capture. In a twist of fate, the investigation into the landlord's son took place just as he was about to be sent to the Poyang prison camp as a supervisor. His transfer coincided with the overhaul of the labor camp, which was rapidly expanding as rural campaigns uncovered or produced new enemies of the revolution. Originally one large unit, the camp was now divided into first, second, and third units. Newly arrested criminals started in the third unit, and through hard work and good behavior they earned transfer into the second and then the first unit, gaining freedom as they moved through the ranks.[43]

In mid-1951 the landlord son had been selected for assignment to the camp's first unit as a junior political instructor.[44] As the case of the Bodhisattva Society came to a close his transfer, career, and very freedom remained in limbo. The documents in Runaway Xu's casefile only hint at Zhu Shuyi's involvement in the case, leaving his final fate unknown. Coincidently, the bureau farm that had played such an important role in the investigation was converted into another labor camp in 1952. There is a chance that Zhu Shuyi ended up there, not as a guard but as a prisoner.

Creating the Case of the Bodhisattva Society

This case, much like the previous two, left me with no shortage of questions. What ever happened to Zhu Shuyi? Was he able to escape the crimes of his father? This investigation contains no mention of any proof that he had helped his father, or even known the whereabouts of the escaped landlords. Only his family ties marked him as a suspect. This I can say with certainty: his dilemma may have been unique in its particulars, but many Chinese citizens found their family ties under attack in the People's Republic. The revolution came not just to town and village, but to the family as well. Everyone would have to pick sides, which meant younger generations often had to distance themselves from their elders. During land reform, countless landlord children would face the choice between family and state.

These landlord children, at least for this moment, had a choice in their role. Would they try to protect their parents and risk accusations that they were holding out for the return of the old Republic? Or would they stand with the masses and repudiate their families for prospering through the exploitation of the peasantry? An unhappy and unfair decision, but in the long run class wasn't a choice, but rather an unavoidable inheritance. When land reform divided village society with class labels, rural citizens could advocate for a class status but in the end had to accept the decisions of work teams and peasant associations. In a cruel twist these class labels became hereditary and were passed on to future generations. These were not neutral roles. There was a reason that the Communists were so wary of Poyang's shrimp opera troupes. Party propaganda relentlessly pushed images of corrupt and lecherous landlords preying on honest and kind peasants. The party's vision of the rural order could never tolerate dissenting views. Security officers, trained to believe that landlords were by nature invested in bringing back the old Republic, were quick to see counterrevolution, even in the traditional operas staged to celebrate harvests and festivals.

That's why despite everything you have read so far, I cannot say with any certainty that the Bodhisattva Society ever existed as a coherent organization. Would Kuang Number Four have known that he wasn't just helping out a troubled relative, but acting on the behalf of an underground network dedicated to overthrowing the People's Republic? It would have been nice to hear from Kuang Number Four. Readers should know that this casefile is filled with reports penned by security officers. For casefiles 1 and 2 we can endlessly question the confessions given by Scholarly Wu and Big Tiger. What kinds of pressure were they under during interrogation? Did they answer truthfully? Did officers just write what they wanted to hear? And so on. There is, of course, no way to definitively answer any of these questions. But despite these lingering uncertainties, their confessions offer echoes of their voices and their truths.

There are no such voices or truths in this casefile. Only the words of security officers, who classified the network of villagers attempting to keep the state out of their family affairs as a reactionary secret society. Not a single witness testified to seeing the men of Likuang Village drinking rooster blood. Was that accusation nothing more than an unconfirmed rumor? And so the conclusion of this case, it seems to this historian, says much more about the cops than the criminals. These guys had their careers to think about. Bureau leaders were mostly outsiders, with no desire to stay in Poyang, which must have seemed worlds away from the provincial capital in Nanchang, to say nothing of stately Beijing or glamorous Shanghai. And even local officers must have longed to rise in the ranks. Revolutionary glory led to promotion. Why not use one's clout to earn a reputation as a fierce advocate for the peasant masses? As we will see in our final case, it would be foolish to underestimate the power of the cadres running things in New China.

CASEFILE 4

MERCHANT ZHA GOES TO COURT

Cast of Characters (in order of appearance)

General Li: Li Fengchun, Nationalist general
Secretary Zhou: Zhou Huamin, party secretary, Fifth District
Comrade Guo: Guo Xue, Secretary Zhou's assistant
Merchant Zha: Businessman and accused spy
Landlord Zhang: Owner of the oil press in Hengxi Township
Judge Jiang: Jiang Beiran: County-chief, Poyang County
Township-chief Cheng: Hengxi Township cadre
Cooperative-chief Huang: Hengxi Township cadre
Chairman Zhang: Hengxi Township cadre
Secretary Hu: Cadre, Sixth District
Liu Jingwen: District-chief, Eighth District; judge, People's Tribunal, Fifth Branch
Prosecutor He: Prosecutor and recordkeeper, People's Tribunal, Fifth Branch
Judge Wang: Judge, People's Tribunal

General Li Terrorizes the Mountains

When the People's Liberation Army marched south toward Poyang in the first months of 1949, back when Zhu Old Six and Xie Old Seven still haunted the mountains, many poor farmers waited with cautious optimism. Might the newly arrived soldiers bring the mountain outlaws to justice? Would the People's Government, in stark contrast to every previous Poyang regime, actually serve the people as the Communists promised? Was it possible that farmers might finally get enough land to prosper? Their wealthier neighbors waited in fear. Those with the will and the necessary capital fled, heading to Hong Kong and points beyond to escape the reach of the Communists and their revolution. Over 800 Poyang folk made their way to Taiwan, where the Nationalists were securing a new bastion to house the Republic.[1] They wanted nothing to do with New China. Alone, General Li Fengchun moved against the tide. While thousands fled in fear, he returned home to Poyang.

Among the military strongmen who stalked the mountains of northern Poyang in the first days of Communist rule, none was more feared than General Li. Compared to him, Old Six and Old Seven were petty thugs. A native of Poyang's own Gangtou Village, which sits aside one of the many rivers flowing down into the lake, Li was now a general in the Nationalists' army. As part of what the Communists would one day call Chiang Kai-shek's "contingency plan," he quietly returned to Poyang in February of 1949, giving him an opportunity to organize local resistance just before the People's Liberation Army arrived. By May General Li had rounded up thousands of men into his newly organized National Salvation Army. In a brazen comparison to the Communists' famed Eighth Route Army, General Li gave his ragtag forces a bold nickname: the Ninth Route Army. As he liked to boast, his army had "one more route" than his foes.[2]

The Ninth Route Army terrorized the Poyang countryside in 1949, attacking newly established governments, ambushing work team encampments, and killing agents of the Communist revolution. The emerging Communist regime did its best to bring order to the chaos. In late April Zhou Huamin, a district-level party secretary, led twenty well-armed cadres out from Jingdezhen to establish an outpost at Xiejiatan, a rural market town in northern Poyang, where General Li's forces were most active.[3] Like most cadres now laying the groundwork for the new order, Secretary

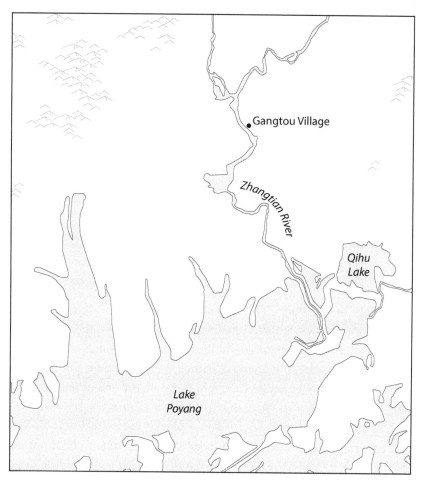

Map 17. Gangtou Village, General Li's hometown.

Zhou was a northerner. Born in faraway Shandong, he joined the party in 1939 and eventually made his way to Henan, where he joined the army of cadres attached to the Second Field Army as it headed south toward Poyang. Assigned to develop what would become the county's Fifth District in Xiejiatan, Secretary Zhou ended up carrying out the revolution in remote villages. Enemies lurked in these mountains, and the Communists considered all of them bandits. Many of these dangerous men were, like Old Six and Old Seven, in fact outlaws. The forces of General Li were something else entirely.

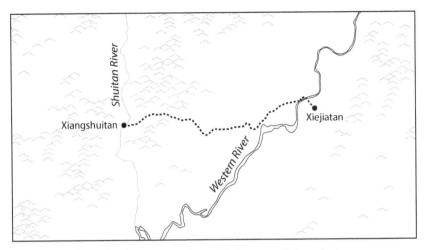

Map 18. Hiking five hours west from Xiejiatan to Xiangshuitan.

On July 11 Secretary Zhou led about a dozen men to Xiangshuitan, a remote mountain community about five hours away by foot. The Communists often traveled these roads, distributing relief supplies, promoting production, and fighting bandits. This time their enemies got the upper hand. Some sixty men under General Li's command ambushed them that day. Eight Communists died, martyred in an elementary school. Secretary Zhou found himself besieged in a blockhouse with Comrade Guo and two young messengers. The four of them were able to hold out and escape back to their outpost in Xiejiatan, which they found deserted: district-chief Shen Guoming had led the rest of his men out in search of Ninth Route Army forces.

Two days later, on the morning of July 13, the Ninth Route Army soldiers unexpectedly appeared in Xiejiatan, determined to finish off the Communists. They succeeded. General Li's men trapped Secretary Zhou and Comrade Guo upstairs in their makeshift headquarters, a commercial shop the Communists had taken over as part of their intervention into the local salt trade. According to local legends, the Ninth Route soldiers taunted Secretary Zhou, demanding he surrender and face a certain execution. A brief exchange of gunfire was followed by a prolonged deadlock. By noon, running low on ammo, Secretary Zhou ordered Guo to make a run for it. Guo handed over his gun and grenades before jumping out the window and dashing to a nearby river. He almost made it: General Li's men shot and killed him midstream. By mid-afternoon, the bandits had enough of waiting and set the commercial shop ablaze. Secretary Zhou, still in his early twenties, perished in the flames. According to the party's official account, the young activist used his final breath to defiantly shout: "Long live the Communist Party! Long live Chairman Mao!"[4]

General Li Is Defeated, Merchant Zha Gets Arrested

The martyrdom of Secretary Zhou occurred during the ferocious summer of conflict between the forces of the old Republic and what would eventually become the People's Republic. The People's Liberation Army arrived in April and by July was aggressively pursuing General Li and his men in the mountains of northern Poyang. Coordinating with local governments and militias, Communist forces smashed the Ninth Route Army. General Li attempted to limit his losses by dividing his forces, but by September his insurrection was truly a lost cause.[5] The Communists captured or killed hundreds of Ninth Route Army men, and took the surrender of hundreds more, alongside a small arsenal of rifles, pistols, hand grenades, swords, and makeshift cannons.

On the run, General Li did his best to lay low in the mountains of northern Poyang, but a People's Liberation Army recon squad tracked him down and captured him alive. The arrest of General Li and his lieutenants, celebrated by the Communists, did little to heal the scars his resistance had brought to Poyang.[6] What of the thousands of men who had joined or otherwise aided the counterrevolutionary Ninth Route Army? Some of them had been captured or killed, but many others returned to their homes and fields and continued their lives as if they had never tried to forestall New China and the liberation of the masses. Hengxi Township, for example, lay only a dozen miles away from General Li's hometown. Surely some Hengxi citizens had helped the rebels. How would new township leaders, installed by Communist work teams, deal with Nationalist collaborators? Could they bring these counterrevolutionaries to justice?

Perhaps they could. On November 15, 1950, over a year after the Ninth Route Army's demise, township cadres finally got Merchant Zha arrested as a "reactionary element." Reading the charges compiled from the testimony of the Hengxi masses, it's hard to imagine such a cruel and

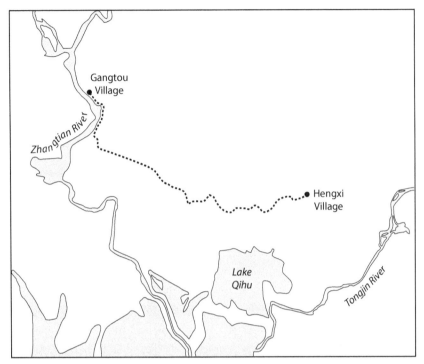

Map 19. The four-hour walk from Gangtou Village (General Li's home-town) to Hengxi Village, seat of Hengxi Township.

petty man. According to a statement issued by the cadres running the Hengxi Township government, this criminal had collaborated with General Li, providing intelligence on the new regime to the forces of counterrevolution. And after the People's Liberation Army crushed the Ninth Route Army, he continued to look for opportunities to engage in guerrilla warfare from Hengxi.

As serious as these charges were, according to Hengxi villagers they represented only a small fraction of Merchant Zha's many crimes. In their portrayal this man, the very definition of an enemy of the people, was certainly worthy of execution by the People's Government. Serving as a military recruiter for the old Nationalist regime, he leveraged the threat of conscription to frighten local families into massive payoffs. He seduced and slept with a married woman. After liberation he attempted to subvert land reform by illegally selling off landlord property, most notably a

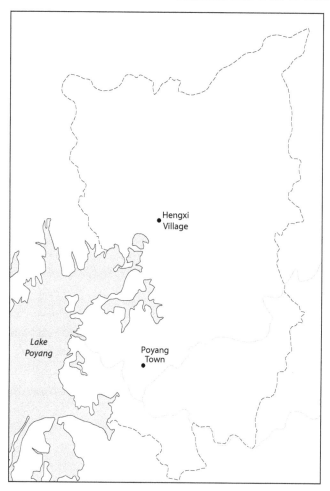

Map 20. Hengxi Village, where Merchant Zha ran into trouble.

huge stockpile of rapeseed kept at a local oil press. Merchant Zha, a man the masses derided as a "reactionary bastard element," had made a huge profit at the expense of the people. The accusation was endorsed by over 200 Hengxi residents, whose names and thumbprints, grouped by lineage in reflection of the centrality of family organizations in the countryside, can still be found in Merchant Zha's casefile.[7]

Arrested and tried for these heinous crimes, Merchant Zha was on track to sharing Big Tiger's fate: a bullet in the head, courtesy of the People's Tribunal. But in the months after his arrest, as his case made its way through the emerging Poyang justice system, something entirely unexpected happened. Despite all the charges levied against him, was it possible that Merchant Zha was in fact an innocent man? The key to this case, the cadres in Poyang Town would eventually realize, hinged on one simple fact: Merchant Zha was an outsider.

Banker Zha Gets Fired

Beyond the fact that he was born in the first years of the old Republic, little is known about Merchant Zha's childhood. Many of the details of his life were hotly contested in the dossier compiled and later archived by Poyang security officers. At the time of his arrest he was a merchant by trade, but he was far more than a businessman. Merchant Zha would himself emphasize that he had a difficult childhood. Originally from nearby Wuyuan County, he studied at a private academy as a boy for five years, only to drop out at the age of thirteen when his father died. With his family now struggling to get by, his education came to an end. He took up farming with his mother until he was twenty-three, when an extended eight-month illness left him too weak to work the fields. But in a few years his earlier education paid off when he found employment with the Wuyuan branch of the Yumin Bank.

Merchant Zha worked at the bank for seven or eight years, but in 1948, at the age of thirty-two, misfortune struck again when his neighbor's house burned down. The fire spread, destroying his own house and his family's entire harvest. Family members scattered, going their own way in search of new livelihoods. Homeless, he made his way east to Poyang in search of another banking job.[8] Merchant Zha, perhaps unknowingly, was at the forefront of the county's push for commercial and industrial modernization. This was a modern bank, run by the Jiangxi provincial government.[9] During the imperial era the town had private money shops, which offered short-term loans for survival, but now modern banks and their valuable banknotes represented a sharp break with tradition. A banking job, even in sleepy Poyang Town, was a promising career path.[10]

Merchant Zha arrived in Poyang County armed with two letters of introduction from his former employers at Yumin Bank. He took a position with the bank's Poyang branch, but left the world of finance after a little over a month. As he later explained, he was let go during a round of layoffs shortly after his arrival. Unemployed, far from home, and chronically misfortunate, he made the first of two very bad decisions, accepting a position in Poyang's Zhegang Township. It was the summer of 1948. Merchant Zha had thrown in his lot with the Nationalists just as they were blundering their way to defeat in their ongoing war with the Communists.[11]

Military Liaison Zha Is Dismissed from Office

Merchant Zha served as the township-secretary in Zhegang for about four months, until early September, when a new post opened up. As luck would have it, the local military liaison had requested a leave of absence to visit his home in Nanchang and never returned.[12] Merchant Zha was appointed in his stead. Despite his background as a failed banker with zero military training, one of his most important responsibilities would be overseeing recruitment efforts, finding men to enlist in the seemingly never-ending war against the Communists.

Conscription had haunted Poyang for decades. Unlike their Communist foes, who proudly boasted of their volunteer army, the Nationalists shamelessly press-ganged men into military service. Back during the war against Japan, Nationalist conscription practices horrified the Americans sent to advise Chiang Kai-shek, including "Vinegar" Joe Stilwell. One of Chiang's fiercest critics, Vinegar Joe compared Nationalist conscription practices to a disaster, only far more regular and deadly: "Famine, flood, and drought compare with conscription like chicken pox with plague." In vivid terms Vinegar Joe described how hapless farmers were abducted from their rice paddies, leaving behind destitute wives and children. Because money could buy freedom, conscription didn't fall on all families equally: "Only office, influence, and money keep conscription out of your house."[13]

In Poyang Nationalist conscription practices followed the corrupt patterns that infuriated Vinegar Joe. In theory, families with only one son were exempt from the draft, which was determined by lottery. Township and hamlet leaders drew bamboo sticks, inscribed with the names of eligible men between the ages of eighteen and forty-five, at random from a cylinder. Unlucky winners were roped off and led into service. Desertion was punished by execution, and some claimed that victims were buried alive. In practice, because military recruitment was often a death sentence, wealthy families bribed officials, ensuring that poor farmers bore the brunt of conscription. As one fictional bandit bemoaned the "bitter truth" of corrupt officials: "With money you can even reach the gods."[14] During the war against Japan, the Nationalists conscripted almost 30,000 Poyang men. The county should have sent even more, but officials typically failed to meet their quotas for new conscripts.[15]

With the Nationalists continuing to conscript Poyang men during the Civil War, Merchant Zha's new post could have been a lucrative one. But like all of his endeavors, it ended in failure before he turned a profit. At the end of 1948 an inspector from the county government reviewed his credentials and discovered what everyone who ever worked with Merchant Zha already knew: he was no military man. Further investigation revealed that he wasn't just unqualified, but had in fact failed to carry out his duties. Stripped of his position and still broke, Merchant Zha couldn't afford to make the journey back home to Wuyuan. Luckily, he convinced the Zhegang township-chief to give him back his old post as township-secretary. And then, in May 1949, the Communists showed up.

Comrade Zha Serves the People

Merchant Zha suddenly found himself working for the Communists at a district office for the new People's Government. The banker turned military liaison had unwittingly become a cadre. He was hardly alone. The Communists encouraged employees of the Nationalist regime such as himself to remain at work and redeem their former sins with good deeds. This request reflected the Communists' desperate need for literate citizens to help manage New China. Keeping employees on board, however, was complicated by the party's inability to pay regular salaries. Working for the People's Government, which was critically short on material goods during these early years, Merchant Zha was compensated according to the provision system. He didn't get paid in cash but in rations of rice and other necessities.[16] Working under the Sixth District based in Hengxi, Merchant Zha was encouraged by district-chief Gao, newly arrived with the Second Field Army, who told Merchant Zha and other holdovers to stay on and become model bureaucrats.[17] In September 1949 a new dis-

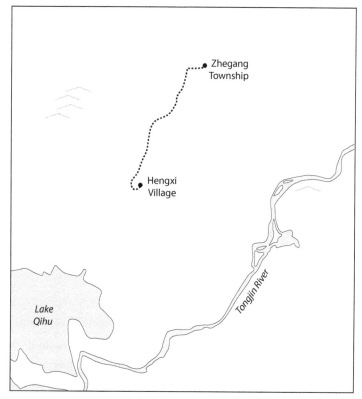

Map 21. A very walkable seventy-five minute trip between Zhegang and Hengxi, both home to government administrations.

trict-chief gave Merchant Zha a post back in Zhegang Township, where he had once served the Nationalists.

A few months later, on January 10, 1950, Jiangxi party leaders expressed concern over the existence of Nationalist Party members and loyalists now working for the People's Government. Might they be plotting against the new regime? Provincial party leaders asked work units to conduct an internal cleansing.[18] Merchant Zha, now working in Zhegang Township, faced the same dilemma that Zhu Shuyi, son of the fugitive Landlord Zhu, had faced while working for the Public Security Bureau: the prospect of an uncomfortable investigation into his past. The landlord son had undergone internal review and kept his job, only to run into trouble after his father broke out of jail. Merchant Zha never went through internal cleansing. Instead, he resigned from his government post on account of illness.[19]

The timing of the illness, just a month after the call to investigate work unit personnel, raises questions. Merchant Zha might have decided that it was best to quit before going through the review process. That way he could avoid having to detail his past duties in the Nationalist administration. Or perhaps he didn't see much economic opportunity in working for the People's Government. Previously, a government post was considered one of the best jobs in the realm. During imperial times, magistrates could count on cash salaries, while their underlings padded their pay with whatever they could squeeze out of locals.[20] No one was getting rich under the People's Government provision system. Or perhaps he was indeed sick. We can only rely on Merchant Zha's own account, in which illness kept him bedridden for over a month. During that time, he later recalled, his mother wrote him and exhorted him to get well and to get back to work so that he could return home to Wuyuan.

Encouraged, Merchant Zha borrowed a load of sesame seeds for capital and teamed up with three Poyang locals looking to make money. The four men had their eyes on the Yitai Oil Press, a local business that had shut down right around the time Merchant Zha left his government post. This was the only oil press in Hengxi Township, so for the men it seemed like a good opportunity to turn a profit while providing an essential product to their neighbors.[21] Earlier, Merchant Zha had found employment with the Nationalists as they were losing the Civil War. Now, just as the Communists were intervening in Poyang's economy, he went into the oil-pressing business. This, his second disastrous choice, set him on a collision course with the executioner's bullet.

Merchant Zha Opens an Oil Press

Commerce and industry, while always overshadowed by agriculture, were alive and well when the Communists came to Poyang. Before the Japanese invaded, Poyang Town's narrow streets and alleyways were crowded with businesses producing and selling a host of products, including porcelain, tobacco, salt, soy sauce, paper, and firecrackers. Including the smallest shops and stands, the town was home to nearly 2,000 commercial enterprises. That number dropped during the war when Japanese bombs put many companies out of business. But the town's economy quickly recovered. Most shops were clustered along the future Liberation Street. Many businesses, especially teahouses, set up shop on River Road. And every morning the farmers and fishermen who lived around Poyang Town brought their goods to market.[22]

The countryside was also home to commerce and had been for hundreds of years. During the reign of the Qianlong emperor, when the final dynasty's commercial glory reached dizzying heights, Poyang merchants hawked their goods at over 300 shops scattered in nineteen large markets, most notably at Stone Gate Street, Old County Crossing, and Forty Mile Street. As the dynasty slowly declined, these markets developed into towns. Jiantian Street, a two-hour walk from Big Tiger's home, started off as a place for villagers to sell felled trees to merchants. The men hauling trees to the marketplace, where about forty households lived, came from a dozen or so villages. By 1912 the town had ten businesses, including an oil press.

In the 1930s 2,000 businesses could be found scattered throughout Poyang's 35 market towns. Stone Gate Street emerged as the most important market town in the county's mountainous north, with over 100 businesses. Other towns were much smaller. At Zhangtian Crossing visitors encountered a solitary main street, two meters wide and constructed from coarse stone. Businesses lined both sides of the way, including a dye shop, a tailor shop, a medicine store, and an oil press. Poyang's rural markets did falter during Japanese invasion. Japanese planes bombed Stone Gate Street. Outlaws briefly seized Hengyong. But rural markets recovered. By the time the Communists arrived in Poyang the county was home to twenty-five market towns and hundreds of businesses.[23]

While his exact thinking remains a mystery, it seems that Merchant Zha was seduced by the opportunities for profit from the Yitai Oil Press, which had stopped production in late February 1950. Landlord Zhang, the owner of the oil press, had given up the business as the revolution came to Poyang villages.[24] Because the press had been sitting idle, no taxes had been paid that year. That was a problem in New China.

Merchant Zha Pays Taxes

The new regime's need for grain and cash had marched cadres and soldiers into the mountains on requisition drives, but that wasn't the only
way the new regime sought to extract resources in Poyang. In May 1949,
almost immediately after establishing the county People's Government,
the southbound cadres set up the all-important Tax Bureau. Bureau cadres hewed to the official policy of continuing to collect established taxes
while amending tax codes to better match the ideals of New China. Tem-
porarily, that included taxes on banquets. Far more important, given the
nature of the local economy, Poyang farmers no longer paying rent on the
fields they now owned would now pay taxes directly to the state. Given
the overwhelmingly agricultural economy, this grain tax largely financed
the county government and its push to improve education and sanita-
tion. But over 15 percent of the county government's income came from
commercial and industrial taxes. In order to facilitate tax collection, the
county established six tax bureau branches in the Poyang countryside,
including an office in Xiaohua that Merchant Zha would soon visit.[25]

Landlord Zhang, the owner of the Yitai Oil Press, was desperate to
find someone to rent out his press and take over the business. With land
reform looming, he wasn't inclined to do business under the Communists.
He had other plans in mind, big plans, and those plans required capital.
Why not rent out the oil press? The only oil production center for miles,
the shop held stores of grain and supplies, and even a team of water buffaloes to power the oil press. Merchant Zha invited three Hengxi locals,
becoming equal partners in a shareholding company, with him as acting
manager.[26] Together they rented the former Yitai Oil Press and reopened
under a new name, the Yongtai Oil Press. Negotiating directly with Landlord Zhang, Merchant Zha and his partners agreed on rental fees for the
oil press and its water-buffalo production team. They also took responsibility for the taxes that were still owed to the People's Government.[27]

Merchant Zha traversed the lake to Nanchang in May 1950 to pay the
oil press's back taxes and opened for business that summer. At the time
it's doubtful he thought much of his time away from Hengxi, but his trip
would eventually raise questions. Where exactly had he gone, and for
what reasons? For as summer turned to fall, the grain and assorted property still held in the oil press attracted the attention of Hengxi peasants.

Not coincidentally, the Communists had recently launched land reform. Villagers wanted to settle accounts with the owner of the oil press, but Landlord Zhang fled Poyang in September. No doubt his recent transaction with Merchant Zha had provided much needed funds as he made his escape. That left the oil press and its healthy stores of raw materials as a potent symbol of his missing wealth, to say nothing of the water buffaloes used to power the oil press. After so many years of war, all farming animals were in short supply. Water buffaloes were so valuable that the new regime used them as prizes to reward labor heroes. One woman won her buffalo after working for seventy-three days without rest to help repair the dikes surrounding Lake Poyang.[28] Right around the time land reform started, Jiang Beiran, the county-chief who sentenced Big Tiger to death, issued a decree outlawing the slaughter of water buffaloes, even old ones. As long as they could eat hay and plow fields, they were protected.[29] And Merchant Zha had a team of water buffaloes. Sitting on so much wealth, all connected to Landlord Zhang, a man now deemed a class enemy, Merchant Zha could hardly go unnoticed once villagers began their land reform campaign.

Three Township Cadres Denounce Merchant Zha

Exactly when the conflict started is uncertain, but the cause of the trouble is clear: the oil press. With the original owner Landlord Zhang nowhere to be found, Hengxi peasants and cadres saw the raw materials now held by Merchant Zha as an irresistible target. According to a later confession from Merchant Zha, the Yongtai Oil Press held millet, lecithin, firewood, sesame seeds, rapeseed, rice, and grain stalks. Earlier in the year Hengxi peasants had come to the oil press seeking to borrow some of this grain. Merchant Zha, almost certainly thinking he would never see any loans returned, refused the request. Now, with land reform in full swing, Hengxi's peasants came to take what they felt rightfully belonged to them. Didn't the Communists say the people were in charge now? Hadn't the peasant masses created this wealth through their own labor? Yet Merchant Zha had legally rented the oil press and paid his taxes. He was confident that he was following Communist policy to focus on production.

From a legal perspective, he had a very strong case. True, peasants often seized landlord property with impunity during the early stages of rural revolution. But more lenient treatment of landlords had become official with the promulgation of the Land Reform Law of the People's Republic of China in the summer of 1950. Landlords would still lose their "five big properties": land, draft animals, agricultural tools, excess grain, as well as any extra housing located within the village. Unlike earlier campaigns, however, landlords would be allowed to keep their other belongings, including all commercial enterprises.[30] The Communists, knowing that rural revolution wreaked havoc on local economies, intended to keep production running smoothly during the first years of New China. That meant not confiscating commercial properties, even when the owners were technically class enemies. But for Hengxi cadres looking for wealth to redistribute to the village poor, the oil press and its stores were an obvious target.

Spurred on by land reform, the new leaders of Hengxi Township moved against Merchant Zha in force. On October 17, 1950, about a dozen men angrily confronted him at the oil press. They were led by three men, recently empowered as township cadres: township-chief Cheng, cooperative-chief Huang, and Chairman Zhang of the peasant association. They had come for the shop's raw materials. Merchant Zha refused, reasoning that these materials belonged to the oil press and were absolutely essential to his business. Didn't the party want to increase commercial production? Didn't the People's Government rely on taxes such as those paid by the oil press? But the three township cadres angrily shut down the shop and sealed off all production materials. Everything that the shareholders had invested in was declared confiscated. This left Merchant Zha and his partners stuck with an oil press that couldn't be returned or used.

Merchant Zha, convinced he was in the right, moved quickly to protect his business. Having served in the Nationalist regime as well as the new People's Government, he knew exactly where to go and headed straight to the county's Industry and Commerce Section. Unfortunately, the section leadership was in the countryside on land reform work teams, so his matter was transferred to the People's Tribunal, which sent him back to his district government, asking that office to use discretion and understanding in his case. Visiting the Sixth District government offices where he had once worked, Merchant Zha told Secretary Hu how the township government cadres had seized the oil press. He then pled for the secretary to pass on this information to the district-chief. Secretary Hu, however, only told him to go back home and cooperate with the township-chief.[31]

Merchant Zha's attempt to go over the heads of township-chief Cheng and his buddies backfired spectacularly. On October 19, the very day that the shareholders tried to reopen their business, the three cadres returned to the press and once again shut it down. This time they even took the team of water buffaloes.

Merchant Zha Goes on the Offensive

A few weeks later, Merchant Zha made his most defiant statement yet. This testimonial, dated November 11, is a remarkable document, filled with the anger of a man firing directly at township cadres in a search for justice. The statement was presented to Liu Jingwen, who was the district-chief over in the Eighth District, headquartered in Forty Mile Street.

Just as county-chief Jiang Beiran played a multiplicity of roles in the county government, Liu Jingwen served in more than one administrative post in his corner of Poyang. Most notably, he was the judge of the Fifth Branch of the People's Tribunal.[32] It was in this capacity that he took Merchant Zha's statement. Merchant Zha signed and affixed his thumbprint to his testimony, as did his three shareholder partners. Another local business owner served as a witness for the statement.

According to "Merchant Zha," as he identified himself, he and his three partners had done everything by the book when they opened the oil press, working closely with the officials in the new regime's Tax Bureau. There was, he insisted, a record of their registration that could prove his claims were true. They had paid the back taxes of the old Yitai Oil Press the very day they reopened the place, personally presenting payment to the comrades in the Tax Bureau. Everything had gone through the Tax Bureau's office in Xiaohua and could be verified. They had gotten permission to reopen.

Linking the three township cadres to the Communists' increasingly common portrayal of exploitative landlords running roughshod over peasants in the dark days before liberation, he repeatedly referred to their actions as *feudal*. Describing what happened when he and his business partners visited the district government, Merchant Zha pointedly noted that they had told everything to Secretary Hu, but because the secretary

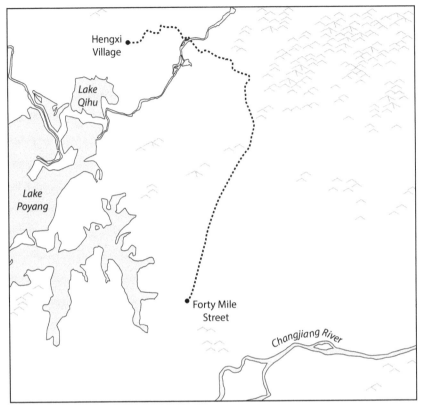

Map 22. The eight-hour hike from Hengxi to Forty Mile Street, home to the Eighth District and the Fifth Branch of the People's Tribunal.

couldn't understand "this kind of feudal behavior," they had been sent back to work it out with the township-chief, who of course was one of the troublesome cadres. They also reached out to the county government in hopes that the Industry and Commerce Section might relieve their suffering by protecting their business so that they could get back to producing oil and paying taxes. According to Merchant Zha, the three township cadres, knowing that they had violated policy and fearing that they had broken the law, used crooked words to vilify the businessmen to the district and county governments.

Merchant Zha further alleged that township-chief Cheng and his leadership group, by shutting down the oil press and laying claim to its production materials, were the real feudal powers in Hengxi. Using the party's own weaponized words to attack the cadres, he claimed his tor-

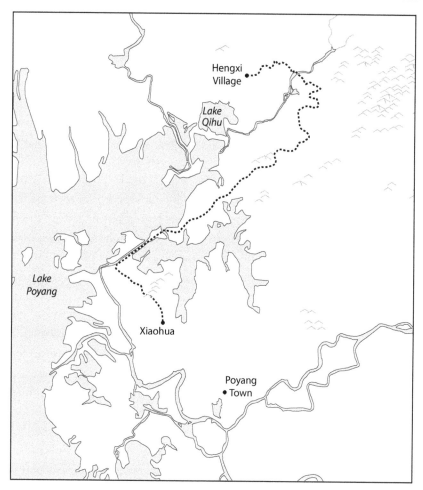

Map 23. The twelve-hour hike from Hengxi to Xiaohua, where Merchant Zha paid his taxes. Given the importance of water transport in Poyang, this trip should have been much quicker than twelve hours.

mentors had used "wicked schemes and methods." Leading a gang of a dozen men, they employed "feudal power" to deceive the masses and "seize" the business. The cadres held "secret meetings," but what they called "guiding the will of the people" was actually "deceiving ignorant peasants" into falsely testifying against Merchant Zha. As for the hundreds of villagers who were in the process of testifying against him, he believed they coveted a share of the stores held in the oil press. Misled by the three cadres during secretive meetings, they had been enticed by promises of profit and blinded by rumors and evil words. The three township cadres, he further alleged, were using the deviant methods of the old regime to "dupe the People's Government above them, and cheat the honest merchants below them."[33]

Merchant Zha defiantly called for nearby townships to investigate the three cadres and their "feudal style of work." Such an investigation would surely bring the facts of the situation to light. The men were not to be trusted. The township-chief was related to the cooperative-chief, who in fact came from a long line of village bosses. From what he had seen from their work style, the three cadres feared nothing, even falsely claiming to have the authority of the district-chief to hold meetings. The three township cadres also used their leverage to keep their corrupt and backward methods secret by stopping Merchant Zha from reporting their ways to the People's Government.[34]

Thanks to the actions of the three cadres, the stockholders couldn't pay their taxes or their workers. The four stockholders, described by Merchant Zha as old friends, had no livelihood and no alternative except to appeal to the People's Government. "I only ask for the government to handle the facts according to the law, safeguard business development and production, and rectify township cadre ideology and profit-seeking style of work, as to avoid businesses ever again suffering from this type of destructive influence." The feudal work style of the township cadres, Merchant Zha noted in closing, could be proven. He pointed first to the mismanagement of the cooperative before turning to the failures of township-chief Cheng back when he was the head of the peasant association. Hadn't over a hundred Hengxi villagers reported him to the county government?[35]

The Masses Demand Justice

Whatever Merchant Zha had hoped to achieve with his defiant statement of innocence failed. He had made his accusations to the Fifth Branch of the People's Tribunal, which was attached to the Eighth District of the People's Government. Liu Jingwen, of course, ran both the court and the government. Just two days later, on November 15, 1950, less than a month after his initial confrontation with the three Hengxi cadres, the

Eighth District of the People's Government turned around and arrested the hapless businessman. For while Merchant Zha appealed to the government, the three cadres made their case directly to the masses. Under their direction the villagers of Hengxi closed ranks and provided unanimous testimony against the outsider from Wuyuan County who dared to question the township's leaders.

As the trial approached, over 200 Hengxi residents came forward to formally accuse Merchant Zha of a litany of crimes. The resulting document is dominated by their red thumbprints, used in lieu of signatures to certify the truth of their complaints, grouped together by lineage. These hundreds of unadorned thumbprints testify to the fact that these accusers were the kinds of poor farmers that the party vowed to liberate: only a handful of them were able to add a red stamp from their personal seal. According to the masses of Hengxi, the businessman was in fact a counterrevolutionary in need of execution to pay for his crimes. A cruel henchman serving the old Nationalist regime, he demanded payoffs by threatening to send Hengxi sons off to war. His crimes continued after the Communists arrived. He plotted with Landlord Zhang, owner of the oil press, to wreck land reform. Sleeping with the man's wife, he had hoped to join Landlord Zhang in his escape from New China. He didn't get away, but he absconded with massive amounts of materials held in the oil press, stealing away to Nanchang to sell the goods for profit. When Hengxi villagers had come to ask to borrow grain, he "verbally abused the masses." He spread rumors all over the place to disrupt land reform and "murder the hearts of the poor."

Most spectacularly, he had conspired with General Li's hated Ninth Route Army, providing them with information about the new regime, leading to many deaths among Poyang's poor farmers. As such, the masses of Hengxi asked for him to be convicted and shot dead. As chief of the Eighth District Liu Jingwen concurred. He sent Merchant Zha to stand trial at a branch of the People's Tribunal, where Liu Jingwen himself would serve as judge. It was time to examine and strictly punish Merchant Zha, district-chief Liu added, to "help the poor have their day of liberation."[36]

Merchant Zha Reflects from Prison

As 1950 came to a close, Merchant Zha sat in jail. On December 15, shortly before going to trial, he made his first "self-reflection letter." In this document, penned on stationery specially printed for criminal confessions, he detailed his personal history, describing how he made his way from Wuyuan to Poyang in search of work. He noted that his was a family that had lived through three generations of poverty, dating back to his grandfather. That should have qualified him as a friend of the revolution. As for the hoopla over the oil press, Merchant Zha pushed the blame on the owner, Landlord Zhang. The man, he said, was "dishonest" and concealed his assets from the public. Explaining his interactions with township-chief Cheng, Merchant Zha softened his earlier tone, calling the decision to seal off the oil press and its assets on October 17 an error in judgment. His trip to the district government was recast as an attempt to get the government to send someone to explain what he and his partners were doing wrong, so they could then change their ways. In closing, the merchant asked for the county government to intervene, still confident that he wasn't at fault.[37]

A few days later, on December 21, Merchant Zha made a second self-reflection, answering pointed questions about the charges the district government had leveled against him. This time he admitted he had erred by not going through the peasant association when he rented the landlord's oil press just prior to the start of Hengxi's land reform campaign. That, he now saw, could be seen as covering up for the landlord. But he was still defiant. Again, he stressed the dishonesty of Landlord Zhang, presenting himself as a victim. As he saw things, the masses only turned on him because he was renting the fled landlord's property. The township government, by shutting down the oil press and confiscating its raw materials, had caused the businessmen extreme financial difficulties. Merchant Zha hadn't been able to pay taxes, nor could he pay his workers. That's why he had no choice but to ask the district government to resolve the conflict, but the district cadres claimed "they couldn't help me solve these problems before land reform."[38] Detailing his work with the township government before the arrival of the Communists, Merchant Zha followed Big Tiger's lead and made sure to note this was a *fake* government. But unlike the man executed as an evil tyrant, he admitted to no crimes while serving the Nationalists. He insisted that he had never harmed the masses.

Discussing his decision to go into business, he highlighted his altruistic motives of providing a much-needed commodity to an area without another oil-production facility. All of his production had stayed local: "Ever since I opened the Yongtai Oil Press for business, I never once rented a boat or cart to transport local produce out of the region." He had records for all of his business relations with the landlord owner of the oil press, and they had both followed proper procedures. Township-chief Cheng's claims to the contrary were untrue. Everything had been filed and approved by the Xiaohua tax office. The three Hengxi township cadres, however, had ignored all of this when they shut down the oil press, not even bothering to work with Merchant Zha and his three partners, only saying what they had done wrong. That was the only reason he had appealed to the Industry and Commerce Section. But the People's Government kept passing his case from one administrative unit to another, only making things worse. In closing he stressed his own suffering, offering the rarest of insights into what it meant to sit in lockup in Poyang: "I only have this one shirt, and I don't have any relatives to deliver a change of clothes. I'm uneasy during the day and can't sleep at night. I ask the government to be lenient and wrap up this case as early as possible, so that I might avoid any further economic difficulty."[39]

Merchant Zha Is Tried by the Branch Tribunal

In January of 1951 Merchant Zha's trial took place at the Fifth Branch of the People's Tribunal. Judge Liu, who also served as the local district-chief, presided over the case. To supplement his two letters of self-reflection, the court directly questioned Merchant Zha. An account of his questioning, stamped with the seal of Prosecutor He, appears in the case file. Prosecutor He served as both prosecutor and recordkeeper during the trial. According to this account, written by the man asking the questions, Merchant Zha discussed his past employment and his social contacts. He denied any charges of corruption stemming from his days as a government employee for the old Republic. Merchant Zha also insisted that he had no ties to the hated General Li. In fact, at the time of the Ninth Route Army attacks he was working for the People's Government under the supervision of district-chief Gao of the Second Field Army. Merchant Zha further explained that he had never been a member of the Big Sword Society, nor had he helped any landlords escape Poyang. He admitted that he knew Landlord Zhang, while also flatly denying that he had slept with the man's wife or helped him conceal any property.[40]

But the charges levied by the masses of Hengxi, confirmed by hundreds of red fingerprints in their formal complaint, couldn't be ignored. In his official ruling, authorized by his personal stamp as well as the official seal of the Fifth Branch of the People's Tribunal, Judge Liu found Merchant Zha guilty of four crimes. First, during his time as military liaison for the old regime he had leveraged the threat of conscription to blackmail the masses and enrich himself. Second, after liberation Merchant Zha gathered intelligence for General Li, spying on People's Liberation Army detachments and hoping to obstruct the new order. Third, after the collapse of the Ninth Route Army, Merchant Zha lived aimlessly in the oil press and concealed Landlord Zhang's grain in a failed attempt to wreck land reform. Fourth, Merchant Zha frequently left town for weeks on end. Exactly where he went was unknown but he was "certainly under suspicion of being a spy." In light of these serious charges, Merchant Zha got off easy with a ten-year sentence.[41] He was lucky that Judge Liu didn't have him shot dead as Hengxi villagers had demanded. But there must have been little joy at the prospect of spending ten years in a labor camp, even if Golden Cao was still there to regale him with stories of his days with the Eastern Mountain Ridge bandits.

Then, almost six months later, the unexpected happened. On June 25, 1951, Judge Wang Shouguo formally reduced the sentence to a year. According to his ruling, the adjusted sentence was in recognition of the fact that Poyang villagers had railroaded Merchant Zha, who after all was an outsider from Wuyuan County: "Because he is from outside of the county, locals framed him as a Ninth Route Army spy."[42] How did the Poyang authorities finally figure out the truth? What of the township leadership that had led the inquisition of Merchant Zha and demanded his execution? Merchant Zha's casefile offers no clues.

Security Officers Send Merchant Zha Home

Because Judge Wang ruled that Merchant Zha had in fact covered up for Landlord Zhang as he scattered his property during land reform, he remained in jail. On January 20, 1952, he made another confession.

This time, without explanation, security officers classed him as a peasant. Given the many years that had passed since Merchant Zha last farmed, this may have been a mistake. But all parties involved seemed to understand why the businessman had been jailed. When asked why he was arrested, he cut to the heart of the matter, never implicating the township authorities of any wrongdoing: he had rented the oil press from a landlord, but refused to hand over the grain the landlord had stored in the business. "I resisted, I refused the confiscation," Merchant Zha lamented from prison. "At that time my mind was confused and blind, and so I refused to admit my error, right up until I was arrested by the county." Even after his arrest he thought the whole thing was a mistake. But this was his only crime. Asked if he had anything else to confess to, he simply said "no."[43]

Exactly five months later, on June 20, 1952, security officers finally set Merchant Zha free. He started that day by making his final confession, once again clarifying the nature of his crimes, all of which involved the oil press. The issue of spying for the Ninth Route Army, which had nearly led to his execution, never even came up once. Here was his true crime: in opening the oil press, he hadn't "gone through the procedures of the masses." The landlord owners never obtained permission to rent out their idle oil press. And because he didn't understand the policy of "the things of the landlords are the property of the people," he didn't even realize he was committing a crime. He further angered locals, first by not dispersing loans and later by not disclosing the grain stored in the business during land reform, thereby inadvertently concealing landlord property. This, he confessed, had indeed hindered land reform. No mention was made of the three township cadres, although Merchant Zha expressed regret for thinking he was innocent and seeking out higher-level authorities for help.[44]

Later that same day, county security officers recommended him for immediate release on parole. According to their review of his case, Merchant Zha was guilty, but only for refusing to hand over landlord property during land reform. Their request was forwarded to the county People's Tribunal. Headed by judges Jiang Beiran and Liu Jingwen, the tribunal ruled that while Zha was indeed guilty of concealing landlord property during land reform, this crime was minor. He had served his sentence. He would be subject to supervision, but otherwise he was a free man.[45] Judge

Liu had served at the branch court that had sentenced Merchant Zha to prison for ten years in early 1951. Judge Jiang, of course, was Poyang's county-chief, and oversaw the local legal system, just as magistrates had done for hundreds of years in the county by the lake. Judge Jiang may have chided or scolded Judge Liu for getting the initial ruling so wrong, but the documents reveal nothing of their conversations.

Releasing Merchant Zha in the summer of 1952, security officers made no mention of the three township cadres who had nearly gotten him executed for crimes he never committed. Instead, their final report, filed on July 24, was a self-congratulation for providing the criminal with a "lenient education" and allowing him to return home. His crime, inadvertently covering up for Landlord Zhang during land reform, was now recognized as not particularly serious. Merchant Zha was officially cleared on the charge of spying for General Li and the Ninth Route Army. Security officers also recognized that Hengxi locals had framed him, yet seemed entirely uninterested in pursuing that matter. Before returning home, Merchant Zha, as Scholarly Wu had done two years earlier, agreed to abide by the eight oaths of the People's Government. He would make a great effort to engage in production, accept the supervision of the people, guarantee to not start rumors, and stay close to the masses. He would never again break the law, sincerely comply with government ordinances, strive to become a person of the new society, and willingly accept the government's strict punishment.[46] With these eight promises, Merchant Zha exited the historical record and returned to obscurity.

Closing the Book on Merchant Zha

Shivering in jail in ragged clothes while far from home, Merchant Zha must have felt that he was living a nightmare. Yes, he had run afoul of the policies of the new regime during the redistribution of wealth that the Communists had made an essential part of their rural revolution. But how could hundreds of his neighbors come forward to claim he had spied for the notorious Ninth Route Army? The businessman had learned a hard lesson. In the upheavals of China's revolution, reality could become entirely divorced from the weaponized words that were everywhere in New China. Over in Gao Village, a Poyang man had been accurately classified as a rich peasant during land reform. During a subsequent campaign to reexamine class labels, a neighbor with a grudge convinced a visiting work team that the rich peasant was actually a landlord. For decades, the unlucky "landlord" and his family suffered no shortage of humiliation.[47]

The Communists didn't invent any of this. The Nationalists had their fair share of false accusations, made deadly through weaponized words. Didn't they dismissively refer to their political rivals as *bandits*? The practice, however, was perfected in the People's Republic. These incidents of slander are most associated with later mass campaigns, especially the Cultural Revolution, when top Communists were felled by baseless accusations of anti-party activity. But the previous cases all suggest that gaps between labels and reality, as well as false accusations, were essential to the revolutionary experience. Old Six and Old Seven: Were they self-interested outlaws? Or were they generals leading an army to restore the Nationalists to power? Big Tiger: According to the charges that got him a bullet in his head, courtesy of county-chief Jiang Beiran, he was a landlord. Oddly he farmed his entire life; there is no record he ever rented out any of his fields. And don't forget Kuang Number Four, the farmer who joined a counterrevolutionary society that he quite possibly never knew existed. What is most unique about Merchant Zha's case is that the scam came from the people at the grassroots. Not coincidentally, he walked free.

And what about the township cadres who tried to get Merchant Zha killed? As Judge Jiang must have known, the three men fabricated a wild story, claiming that the man from Wuyuan was a notorious war criminal who deserved to be executed. They had used their position of authority in Hengxi to mislead local farmers into joining their plot, a ruse that almost ended with the execution of an innocent man. Nothing is said of their fate in Merchant Zha's casefile. Perhaps they lost their leadership roles, but during these years cadres were seldom punished for having an overzealous approach to rural revolution. They may have been promoted. Even if they got in trouble for their actions, that they came so close to getting an innocent man killed shows the power of rural cadres in the People's Republic. If we believe Merchant Zha, the three men were little more than bullies, ruling over their neighbors with an iron fist. Three Big Tigers, now backed by the Communists instead of the Nationalists.

As a historian, there are many lessons to be found in the bewildering tale of Merchant Zha, but none seem more important than the power of village cadres. I have had the good fortune to travel throughout the Chinese countryside and meet a few local leaders. I'm happy to report that thoughtful and conscientious cadres exist, and they are indeed valued by their communities because they truly do want to improve the lives of their neighbors. The types of cadres that nearly got Merchant Zha killed also existed. They would make life miserable for the villagers unlucky enough to be under their rule for decades. The disasters of those years, especially the famines of the Great Leap Forward, can be only understood within the context of their local clout. Still, I shouldn't get ahead of myself. All of this still lay in the future. On June 20, 1952, Merchant Zha walked out of jail a free man. I don't have a clue what happened to him next, but I know he had a say in his final fate.

A FEW MORE WORDS
IN CLOSING

The way from archive to history is not a fixed path. Consider this: writing this book, I decided to transform each of the four casefiles into individual narratives. I did so because I wanted to delve as deeply as possible into each casefile and reveal what rural revolution meant for the people who got tangled up in the legal system of the People's Republic. But I could have chosen a different route and combined the cases into a single narrative, proceeding chronologically through the arrival and implementation of rural revolution in this corner of the Chinese countryside. That story would still begin in 1949, but with General Li, who didn't show up in this book until casefile 4. In truth, he got to Poyang in February, two months before the Communists arrived and well before the northern cadres celebrated the county's liberation on May 1.

Then came the chaotic and violent summer of 1949. In June Golden Cao and his gang of outlaws murdered a platoon of soldiers in Xiejiatan before fleeing to the east to link up with Zhu Old Six and Xie Old Seven. On July 4 three landlords first plotted the assassination of Comrade Zhou in Dayuan Village. That very night Boss Wang led his Big Swords in a deadly attack on the work team stationed alongside the Hengyong Dam. The following day Old Six and Golden Cao ambushed a platoon of soldiers at Pig Mouth Mountain, martyring most of them on the spot. Emboldened, the next morning Old Seven led a disastrous charge on the Communist outpost at Chuanwan. Just a few hours later, the three Dayuan landlords invited Big Tiger to share a meal and discuss a murder. Two days later, late in the evening of July 8, Big Tiger led his assassination squad up to Dayuan Village. Comrade Zhou never saw the dawn.

The bloodshed of that first summer of New China dissipated as the Communists dispatched the People's Liberation Army to drag their enemies down from the mountains. With peace came the establishment of the People's Government, built on the corpse of the old Republican county regime. Many bureaucrats remained on the job. As fears about these holdover employees increased in early 1950, provincial leaders called for an internal cleansing of all work units. Zhu Shuyi stayed with the Public Security Bureau even though his father was a landlord. Merchant Zha, in contrast, left his position with the People's Government to open an oil press. In March the county established its People's Tribunal, just in time for the launch of a campaign against evil tyrants. As part of that campaign, Filial Zhou tried and failed to get Big Tiger arrested for the murder of his father. In July security officers took a final confession from Scholarly Wu as they attempted to unravel the origins of counterrevolution in the countryside. His statement, which suggests that he was about to regain his freedom, brings his casefile to a close.

As summer turned to fall, with land reform underway, rural revolution started heating up. In October three township cadres angrily confronted Merchant Zha over the stores of grain in his oil press. The following month, fears of counterrevolution pushed national leaders to call for an all-out investigation into the enemies they believed to be lurking everywhere. The combination of rural revolution and paranoia over counterrevolution affected all three of the still-ongoing investigations. Merchant Zha went down first, arrested on November 15. Four days later Landlord Hua, head of the Bodhisattva Society, was detained as well. And on December 11 Big Tiger was finally arrested for the murder of Comrade Zhou. Despite the severity of his crime, his initial conviction at a branch of the People's Tribunal only resulted in a limited prison term.

A different branch of the People's Tribunal found Merchant Zha guilty of spying for General Li in early 1951, just about a month before the Bodhisattva Society men broke out of jail. In March Judge Jiang Beiran overruled Big Tiger's initial verdict and sentenced Big Tiger to death; three months later another judge realized that Merchant Zha was innocent of nearly all the charges levied against him by the three cadres running his township. On July 9 Runaway Xu turned himself in to the Political Defense Section and went undercover as a secret agent. Thanks to his work, exactly one month later security officers arrested the ringleaders of the Bodhisattva Society. I assume these men were executed, but their fates remain unconfirmed as their casefile comes to an end. Throughout 1951 both Big Tiger and Merchant Zha sat in jail. Their casefiles didn't end until the following year. On April 28 Big Tiger was shot dead for his crimes. Merchant Zha walked free less than two months later.

Read collectively, the tales told in this book reveal the methodological arrival of state power at the grassroots level. Through a punishing combination of revolutionary campaigns, legal investigations, and sheer patience, the northern cadres in Poyang Town brought state power to villages in never-before-seen ways. Far too many died along the way: some martyred, others executed. This is what the revolution looked like at the grassroots. To be sure, the Communists never found an answer for local reverence for family and religion. And some found ways to continue to defy the new order well after the events covered in this book. One particularly stubborn band of Jiangxi outlaws held out until 1958.[1]

But for those who had prospered under the old regime, the establishment of the People's Republic was nothing less than an extinction-level event. This sea change began with pitched battles between the People's Liberation Army and armed locals like Old Six and Old Seven. Then the Communists quickly brought their revolution to every corner of the countryside. Local bosses who had abused their power, men such as Big Tiger, were brought to justice through mass campaigns against evil tyrants. Land reform work teams promoted new rural leaders and redistributed land. Organizing poor farmers, work teams uncovered exploitation, abuse, and even betrayals long concealed. Villagers attempting to shield their own from the Communists and their courts faced an impossible task. Peasant associations, deftly linking rural society to the People's Government, weren't going anywhere. Neither were the officers who cracked the case of the Bodhisattva Society. There was, of course, no shortage of injustice as the new order came to power. Didn't Merchant Zha get railroaded by township cadres, who saw him as a troublesome outsider? Yet even the most hardened critic of the Communist Party must note that Merchant

Zha, unlike Big Tiger, avoided the executioner's bullet and eventually walked free.

I wrote this book to investigate the arrival of New China in one small corner of a vast countryside. Relying on a fractured and contradictory set of documents, I endeavored to recreate the clash of orders old and new in Poyang. Given the nature of my sources, I'm positive that I made a few errors along the way. The security officers who investigated counter-revolution in Poyang villages are unreliable narrators. Thanks to their ideological training and their concerns about their careers, we have good reason to question their reports. And the documents they left behind aren't just incomplete, but riddled with contradictions and mistakes as well. Every promise of hearing directly from rural citizens comes with the peril of the inevitable distortion of the casefiles and their textual echoes. But I'm also sure the sources contain much truth. I know that when push came to shove, Scholarly Wu chickened out and refused to join the march on the government offices in Chuanwan. Big Tiger most certainly did help kill Comrade Zhou, and as a result he was shot dead by the Communists. Runaway Xu leveraged everything he knew about other fugitive land-lords to save his own skin. And three township cadres coldly blackmailed Merchant Zha for daring to question their newly won authority, not that anyone really seemed to care.

What really strikes me, and I suspect that many readers will agree, is how many questions we are all left with as this book comes to a close. Whatever happened to Boss Wang after he tucked his tail between his legs and returned home to Anhui? Did the Communists ever let Golden Cao out of that labor camp, or did they put a bullet in his head once his case finally came to a close? What about Comrade Hou, the man Big Tiger's assassin squad left for dead? I have three questions for his casefile. Why was he in Dayuan Village that night? How did he possibly survive the brutal assault? And why didn't he or a family member return to Poyang to seek justice and compensation?

Moving on, were the members of the Bodhisattva Society really going to risk capture and launch an uprising before fleeing Poyang? If the au-dacious and talented security officers who broke this case invented that detail of their investigation, what else did they imagine? After all, not a single witness testified to seeing anyone drink a drop of rooster-blood wine. And whatever came of Merchant Zha after he was released from prison? Did his luck finally change? Did he get back to Wuyuan County? I also wonder about those three township cadres. They clearly committed more than one crime when they ginned up such outlandish charges against an innocent man.

Having stared at these four casefiles for a few years now, I have come to peace with the fact that these truths will never be known. I hope readers will forgive me for telling incomplete stories. Perhaps peering into this world long lost will temper the frustration of unanswered questions. If not, readers should understand that in the process of working on this book I discovered that the kinds of sources I used, while a tremendous challenge to find, exist in far greater abundance than I had ever dared hope. Despair over what we don't know is a poor substitute for the fascination for the many stories that are still waiting to be told. The leaders of the People's Republic of China, from Mao Zedong to Xi Jinping, have long prided themselves as master storytellers. Seldom do they welcome others, particularly outsiders, to tell these stories. Much better to dictate the narrative and decide what is fake and what is true. But I'm deeply suspicious of any attempt to control narratives of the past. I have been working with historical documents for decades now, ever since my own days as an undergraduate student. What I learned then is just as true now: history lives at the intersection of our sources and our narrative instincts. That means the past is, by its very nature, open to interpretation. All one needs to get started is a document and a story to tell.

FURTHER READING

The Setting: The County by the Lake

Poyang, in most respects a rather typical place, has benefited from a surprising amount of scholarship on the county and its history. By a remarkable turn of events during the Cultural Revolution, Mobo Gao, born to a poor peasant family, was given the chance to attend university. Professor Gao now teaches Chinese Studies in Australia and has written two book-length studies of his home village: *Gao Village: Modern Life in Rural China* (Honolulu: University of Hawaii Press, 1995) and *Gao Village Revisited: The Life of Rural People in Contemporary China* (New York: Columbia University Press, 2019). For more on the kinds of documents used in this book, see Shigu Liu, "Using Local Public Security Archives from the 1950s—Poyang County, Jiangxi," in *Fieldwork in Modern Chinese History: A Research Guide*, edited by Thomas David DuBois and Jan Keily (New York: Routledge, 2020).

My description of Poyang's rocky course through modern Chinese history is far too brief to capture the complexities of rural revolution. For a more detailed investigation see the two studies penned by Edward Freidman, Paul Pickowicz, and Mark Selden on Wugong Village: *Chinese Village, Socialist State* (New Haven, CT: Yale University Press, 1993) and *Revolution, Resistance, and Reform in Village China* (New Haven, CT: Yale University Press, 2005). For a broader view of agrarian change, see Philip Huang, *The Peasant Economy and Social Change in North China* (Stanford, CA: Stanford University Press, 1988). And if you don't have time for these books, at least read Joseph W. Esherick, "Ten Theses on the Chinese Revolution," *Modern China* 21, no. 1 (January 1995).

This overview of Poyang's history made frequent references to the grassroots. Readers should know that this seemingly innocuous description is a loaded term. In the study of the recent Chinese past, "grassroots history" is an informal category of scholarship, typically characterized by the use of locally produced documents to explore the realities of everyday life. But how can we use the minutiae of lived experiences to explain broader historical change? That's a good question to ponder as we explore the four casefiles. See Jeremy Brown and Matthew D. Johnson, "Introduction," *Maoism at the Grassroots* (Cambridge, MA: Harvard University Press, 2015), and Elizabeth J. Perry, "The Promise of PRC History," *Journal of Modern Chinese History* 10, no. 1 (January 2016).

Casefile 1: Bandits, Big Swords, and the Rebel Scholar

This casefile peers into some of the hardest-to-access corners of Chinese society. For more on banditry before the establishment of the People's Republic, see Philip Billingsley, *Bandits in Republican China* (Stanford, CA: Stanford University Press, 1988). For more on the origins of the Big Swords, and how they factored into anti-Christian violence, see Joseph W. Esherick, *The Origins of the Boxer Uprising* (Berkeley: University of California Press, 1987). For a closer look at secret societies, see Di Wang, *Violence and Order on the Chengdu Plain: The Story of a Secret Brotherhood in Rural China, 1939–1949* (Stanford, CA: Stanford University Press, 2018).

For more on the labor camp system see Philip F. Williams and Yenna Wu, *The Great Wall of Confinement: The Chinese Prison Camp through Contemporary Fiction and Reportage* (Berkeley: University of California Press, 2004), and Jan Kiely, *The Compelling Ideal: Thought Reform and the Prison in China, 1901–1956* (New Haven, CT: Yale University Press, 2014).

Casefile 2: Big Tiger, Tyrant of the Mountain

Big Tiger's case serves as a useful starting point for a deep dive into the rich field of Chinese legal history. For criminal law, see Klaus Mühlhahn,

Criminal Justice in China: A History (Cambridge, MA: Harvard University Press, 2009). For civil law, see Philip Huang, *Chinese Civil Justice, Past and Present* (Lanham, MD: Rowman and Littlefield, 2010). For examples of how much legal casefiles can offer historians of the People's Republic, see Yang Kuisong, *Eight Outcasts: Social and Political Marginalization in China under Mao*, translated by Gregor Benton and Ye Zhan (Berkeley: University of California Press, 2019), and Daniel Leese and Puck Engman, editors, *Victims, Perpetrators, and the Role of Law in Maoist China: A Case-Study Approach* (Berlin: De Gruyter, 2020).

This casefile highlights how class labels were often inaccurately applied to Chinese citizens. Despite the class label handed to him, Big Tiger was no landlord. But social classes, including landlord households, did exist in the countryside: the documents in the casefile provide ample evidence that some households were much wealthier than their neighbors. For a broader look at class, see Felix Wemheuer, *A Social History of Maoist China: Conflict and Change, 1949–1976* (Cambridge: Cambridge University Press, 2019).

Ms. Zhao played a pivotal role in Big Tiger's fall, but far too little about her is said in the casefile. She fits into the pattern seen in Neil Diamant's study of the Marriage Law: poor peasant women were the most likely to file for divorce. See Neil J. Diamant, *Revolutionizing the Family: Politics, Love, and Divorce in Urban and Rural China, 1949–1968* (Berkeley: University of California Press, 2000). Without a doubt the most disappointing discovery in the casefiles was the absence of female voices. For a much-needed corrective, see Gail Hershatter, *The Gender of Memory: Rural Women and China's Collective Past* (Berkeley: University of California Press, 2011).

Casefile 3: The Case of the Bodhisattva Society

I have been arguing for years that land reform represented the most significant mass campaign in rural China, the moment when the revolution truly arrived. I even wrote a book about it: Brian DeMare, *Land Wars: The Story of China's Agrarian Revolution* (Stanford, CA: Stanford University Press, 2019). When it was published *Land Wars* was the first book on land reform in decades, but it was quickly followed by three excellent books on the campaigns: Julia Strauss, *State Formation in China and Tai-*

wan: Bureaucracy, Campaign, and Performance (Cambridge: Cambridge University Press, 2019); Matthew Noellert, *Power over Property: The Political Economy of Communist Land Reform in China* (Ann Arbor: University of Michigan Press, 2020); and Jeffery A. Javed, *Righteous Revolutionaries: Morality, Mobilization, and Violence in the Making of the Chinese State* (Ann Arbor: University of Michigan Press, 2022).

It is hard to miss the deep reverence Poyang villagers had for their gods. The documents found in this casefile, however, dismiss all religious beliefs as superstition. For a nuanced look at rural religious practices, including village bodhisattvas and the clash of religion and the state, see Thomas David DuBois, *The Sacred Village: Social Change and Religious Life in Rural North China* (Honolulu: University of Hawai'i Press, 2005).

Two events discovered in this casefile were exceedingly rare, but of such interest that they both warrant further reading. The first was the jailbreak, which allowed the two landlords months of freedom before they were brought to justice. For perhaps the only known prison escapee to truly find freedom, see Xu Hongci, *No Wall Too High: One Man's Daring Escape from Mao's Darkest Prison*, translated and edited by Erling Hoh (New York: Sarah Crichton Books, 2017). The second rare event was the county Public Security Bureau using Runaway Xu as an undercover spy. The Public Security Bureau did use "insiders," but almost always in cities. For more on urban undercover work, see Michael Schoenhals, *Spying for the People: Mao's Secret Agents, 1949–1967* (Cambridge: Cambridge University Press, 2013).

Casefile 4: Merchant Zha Goes to Court

The extreme brutality of General Li's fight against the Communists in the northern mountains only makes sense within the context of the larger conflict: the Chinese Civil War. For a comprehensive overview of this, the final chapter in the showdown between the Nationalists and the Communists, see Odd Arne Westad, *Decisive Encounters: The Chinese Civil War* (Stanford, CA: Stanford University Press, 2003).

Merchant Zha's unfortunate encounter with the legal system highlights the power of local cadres. For just how dangerous cadres could be to their fellow villagers, see Ralph Thaxton, *Catastrophe and Contention in Rural China: Mao's Great Leap Forward Famine and the Origins of*

Righteous Resistance in Da Fo Village (Cambridge: Cambridge University Press, 2008).

Merchant Zha, of course, was only one of many Chinese citizens to stew away in jail due to false accusations. Some foreign friends of the Chinese Communist Party also got to experience this aspect of the revolution. For one such account, see Sidney Rittenberg, *The Man Who Stayed Behind* (Durham, NC: Duke University Press, 2001).

Readers may be curious to learn more about what happened in village China after land reform and the rural campaigns discussed in this book. The short answer is that the Communist Party, after giving fields to farmers in dire need of more land, promptly took the land back in a process of forced collectivization, culminating in the formation of massive communes. For the rounds of collectivization that immediately followed land reform, see Xiaojia Hou, *Negotiating Socialism in Rural China: Mao, Peasants, and Local Cadres in Shanxi, 1949–1953* (Ithaca, NY: Cornell East Asia Series, 2016). For the rise and fall of the commune system, see Joshua Eisenman, *Red China's Green Revolution: Technological Innovation, Institutional Change, and Economic Development Under the Commune* (New York: Columbia University Press, 2018).

ACKNOWLEDGMENTS

My first thanks go to Cao Shuji, professor of history at Shanghai Jiaotong University. I first heard of Professor Cao through Philip Huang, my PhD advisor back at UCLA. As I quickly learned, Professor Cao was busy reshaping the study of rural China by reimagining how scholars might access county archives. His brilliant work has made him a hero to many historians, myself included.

Further thanks to the many colleagues who took the time to talk with me about the county by the lake. That starts with Mobo Gao, whose close reading of his home village provided an ideal introduction to all things Poyang. I was thrilled to also chat Poyang Studies with William Hurst, Wankun Li, Shigu Liu, Chenxi Luo, Juan Wang, and Man Zhang. All of these conversations took place during the long isolation of pandemic lockdown, making each chat essential to not just my research, but my mental health as well. Other colleagues who offered wise words as I worked my way through the casefiles include Jeremy Brown, Thomas Dubois, Joseph Esherick, Matthew Johnson, Tobie Meyer-Fong, Yi Ren, Michael Schoenhals, Amanda Shuman, Ralph Thaxton, Dale Wright, and Jiayan Zhang.

A special thanks to the kind conference organizers who invited me to bring my research to new audiences. In 2018 Jennifer Altehenger and Aaron Moore flew me out to London for their "How Maoism Was Made" conference. The following year Rebecca Karl, Jan Kiely, and Laikwan Pang invited me to Hong Kong for their conference on "Conjuring the Socialist Rural." The feedback I received from my two presentations, to say nothing of the conversations over coffee and dinners, proved invaluable.

This is my second publication with Stanford University Press, and I came back for a reason. The book was in good hands from start to finish.

From the editorial side, Marcela Maxfield oversaw much of the project, and her enthusiasm for the book encouraged me to keep writing. Dylan White shepherded the project to publication, providing wise council on many difficult decisions. Tim Roberts, who worked with me on *Land Wars*, returned as production editor, and I was grateful to once again have him oversee the final stages of production. Knowing her passion for history and attention to detail, I turned to Drew Pearson to index the book, and I thank her for her careful work. Further thanks to Therese Boyd, Lizzie Haroldsen, Sunna Juhn, Kevin Barrett Kane, and David Zielonka.

Thanks to the pandemic lockdown, I wrote every word of this book from my adopted home of New Orleans. It's an odd place to write about rural China, but I have a tremendous support network here at Tulane. Throughout the entire process of research, writing, and production, the School of Liberal Arts provided generous funds that made this book possible. In the History Department Susan McCann and Daniely Soriano solved all my administrative problems. I owe an extra thanks to three faculty members for providing much support during my years of service as the department's Director of Undergraduate Studies. Roseanne Adderley was an oracle of wisdom. Katie Edwards recruited so many history majors. And Karissa Haugeberg did me the biggest favor of all by taking over this thankless bureaucratic post.

As Director of Undergraduate Studies, I always made sure to congratulate new majors for joining a department that believes in faculty-student collaboration. It wasn't just talk. Three exceptional students worked with me on the casefiles: Yingying Cheng, Xiaoyu Yu, and Ziyan Zhang. Our conversations, full of wonder and curiosity, encouraged me to bring the process of archival discovery onto the page. Colin Boyd and Sophia Horowitz scoured for English-language documents, unearthing surprising finds that added another layer of complexity to my understanding of Poyang. The work of these research assistants at the start of the project was echoed by the dozens of students who carefully read and commented on the book as it slowly evolved. Having heard me praise Xunzi for teaching us to accept criticism, they were more than happy to tell me what I was doing wrong. Among my students I owe a special thanks to Grayson Dinovitz, Kai Kwiatkowski, and Brett Rodos.

This book is dedicated to Nina and Miles. These two brave souls walked beside me for every step of the journey. In the summer of 2019 we witnessed history on the streets of Hong Kong. Together, we welcomed friends and family to celebrate Mardi Gras in early 2020. Then the pandemic found New Orleans and the world flipped upside down. We grieved the tragic passing of Donna Denneen. We huddled together as the eye of Hurricane Zeta flew directly above our heads, wondering if the roof was going to fly off. It didn't, but by then my beard had really started to turn grey. Then a few months later, in the summer of 2021, we found ourselves swimming with honu off the North Shore of Oahu, and it seemed like things just couldn't get any better. And then, just a few weeks ago, Hurricane Ida came along and shook things up one last time, just for the hell of it. From start to finish, I lived inside a bubble of aloha so formidable that I never once feared for my sanity. All thanks to Nina and Miles.

NOTES

The Setting

1. This includes Gao Village, studied in depth by Mobo Gao, himself a Poyang local. According to Gao, the process of the lake's destruction really started in the 1970s. See Mobo C. F. Gao, *Gao Village Revisited: The Life of Rural People in Contemporary China* (New York: Columbia University Press, 2019), 37.

2. Wade Shepard, *Ghost Cities of China: The Story of Cities without People in the World's Most Populated Country* (London: Zed Books, 2015), 165.

3. In Chinese: "*shan huan dongbei, shui hui xinan.*" The county is shaped like an upright, if imperfect, rectangle. Measuring 72.8 kilometers from east to west and 90.2 kilometers from north to south (4,214.68 square kilometers), Poyang is over twice as large as Luxembourg, or about the same size as the state of Rhode Island. This and much of the background information on Poyang found in this book comes from Poyang County's official gazetteer, a gigantic two-volume collection that details the county's history in detail. Among the gazetteers I've used over the years, this is one of the best in terms of depth and breadth of coverage. I don't blame the publishers for the decision to use a photograph of birds flying over Lake Poyang's vast waters for the cover of the collection. But from a historian's perspective the lake is just about the most uninteresting thing about Poyang. *Poyang xian zhi* (Beijing: Fangzhi chubanshe, 2010), 1.

4. For readers interested in a more detailed history of Poyang, the region began to attract the attention of outsiders as early as the Warring States era, a time when what we now call China was divided up into a multiplicity of small kingdoms, each vying for supremacy. Between 500 and 300 BCE, Poyang belonged to a succession of kingdoms as their fortunes rose and fell. During the Warring States the region was known as Po, although the character used at the time is now pronounced Pan. Po passed between Chu, Wu, and Yue, three of the most famous kingdoms of the era. Originally part of Chu, Po was first seized by the kingdom of Wu. Later, King Goujian of Yue, who

famously "slept on brushwood and tasted gall" to remind him of his humiliation at the hands of the King Fuchai of Wu, crushed his rival and added Po to his growing kingdom. But as the number of kingdoms dwindled, it was the revitalized Chu state that controlled Po during the final decades of the Warring States era. The kings fighting over Lake Poyang and its shores were regional strongmen who relied on extended family networks to rule their states. Eventually one of these kings conquered his foes and declared himself emperor. The elimination of rival states and the subsequent establishment of the Qin dynasty in 221 BCE marked the start of the imperial era. The founder of that dynasty was only the first of many emperors who would project power from distant throne rooms down to the shores of Lake Poyang, all the better to defend the realm and collect taxes from local farmers, artisans, and merchants. Like all those who followed him, be they emperors or revolutionaries, he relied on bureaucrats to get the job done. The First Emperor divided his realm into thirty-five commanderies. The Jiujiang Commandery, headquartered on the northern banks of the Yangtze, governed Po and six other newly created counties. Readers interested in knowing more about the county's past are encouraged to start with the timeline found here: *Poyang xian zhi*, 8–14.

5. The First Emperor entrusted Wu Rui to represent him in Po. Wu Rui was a formidable local with a lineage that stretched back to some of the most famous kings of the Warring States era. He traced his lineage back to the kings of Wu, including the famous King Fuchai, who had so humiliated King Goujian and drove him to vengeance. Wu Rui's father had served as minister of war for the Chu kingdom, until he fell from favor and was banished to Po. This was the territory Wu Rui would now govern on behalf of the First Emperor. The term used for "magistrate" during his rule was *xianling*. According to Poyang lore, the Lord of Po enlightened his subjects and, very important in the water-soaked lands astride the lake, was quick to provide disaster relief. See the biography of the "Lord of Po" in *Poyang xian zhi*, 266.

6. The magistrates who followed the Lord of Po were not locals. Learning that officials posted to their native places were most likely to enrich their relatives, deviate from their imperial instructions, or perhaps even rise in rebellion, imperial states used the "law of avoidance": magistrates had to be outsiders. This helped magistrates and other bureaucrats avoid entanglements as they implemented the will of the imperial state in Poyang. There were multiple terms used for magistrate, including *xianling*, *zhixian*, and *zhishi*. Judge Fan wasn't magistrate of Poyang County but a *zhizhou*, senior provincial government official. The final dynasty, the Qing, dispatched ninety-six magistrates to Poyang over the course of its long history. For a list of magistrates see *Poyang xian zhi*, 421–24.

7. The first census on record, taken shortly after the Battle of Lake Poyang during the early years of the Ming dynasty, counted 41,210 households and 211,150 subjects in the county. The final census taken in the imperial era, taken in 1869 when the Qing dynasty and the imperial era itself was

well into its slow decline, counted 110,039 households and 846,124 subjects. The Qing dynasty numbers list households and *ding*, men eligible for labor service. These numbers are to be taken as rough estimates. *Poyang xian zhi*, 150. As of 2017 the county was the largest in Jiangxi, with over 1.5 million residents. Gao, *Gao Village Revisited*, 201.

8. For how imperial yamens operated see Bradley Reed, *Talons and Teeth: County Clerks and Runners in the Qing Dynasty* (Stanford, CA: Stanford University Press, 2000).

9. A year later the Catholics of Poyang built a new church. Soon priests and nuns from France, Italy, and the United States found their way to Poyang Town. *Poyang xian zhi*, 200.

10. Sun Yat-sen's seemingly simple approach to Chinese nationalism would cause no shortage of questions. Who, for example, could be defined as "Chinese"? The answer to that question would change after the Manchus were removed from power.

11. According to Poyang historians, in 1926 Chiang Kai-shek appointed Jiang Bozhang to serve as a committee member of the Financial Affairs Council (*caiwu weiyuanhui*). He was also selected to represent Jiangxi at the Nationalist Party Second Representative General Assembly and was given roles in the provincial government. In addition, he found time to teach literature and history at his alma mater, Poyang Academy. For more, see his biography: *Poyang xian zhi*, 289–90.

12. During these years, county magistrates were no longer chosen by emperors but by the regional militarists that the two revolutionary parties had joined together to defeat. Two of the final three magistrates in Poyang before the arrival of the Northern Expedition were Jiangxi men; the third was from neighboring Anhui Province. *Poyang xian zhi*, 424.

13. In 1921 one had destroyed local dikes to flood advancing troops, bringing much destruction to farmlands. "In the Yangtse Valley. III—Hankow and the British Surrender," *Irish Times*, May 3, 1927, 11.

14. Three regiments from the Second Army, Fifth Division of the National Revolutionary Army arrived in Poyang Town in mid-November. Lin Quanfan used the old title *zhishi*; Li Baijia used the modern title *xianzhang*.

15. This Machiavellian turn on his erstwhile allies shocked many in Chiang's own party, cleaving the Nationalists in two. Many conservatives supported Chiang's move and pressed for more purges, but a strong left wing of the party hoped to salvage the United Front. Following Chiang's lead in Shanghai, conservative elements among Poyang Nationalists started moving against local Communists, reaching out to allies in Nanchang, perhaps through Jiang Bozhang, for support. In response Li Xinhan went on the offensive, directing his men in the county Security Regiment to arrest a dozen or so power holders. Charging the men as "local bullies," Li moved to put the men on trial for exploiting and abusing the Poyang masses. The wife of one of the arrested men visited Li at night, carrying two bags filled with gold, silver,

and jewelry. Li refused the bribe and had the accused men executed after a public trial the following day. Li Xinhan's revolutionary justice reverberated through the county but did not reflect the true balance of power between the two parties. *Poyang xian zhi*, 300–301.

16. This wasn't the only change forged in the crucible of April 12. For Communist Party leaders, the Shanghai Massacre revealed the dire need for their own army. They got one on the first day of August, when several thousand soldiers and cadres, nominally under the Nationalists, seized Nanchang, just across Lake Poyang, for the Communists. In later years, the Nanchang Uprising of 1927 would become heralded as the birth of the Communists' famed Red Army, but there was very little to celebrate on that day. The newly formed Red Army was quickly routed by Nationalist forces and forced to leave Nanchang and Jiangxi altogether. As Stephen C. Averill has aptly put it, this was "in fact a poorly planned, last-ditch attempt" by the Communists to "reverse the rising tide of reaction that threatened to swamp the Great Revolution." Stephen C. Averill, "Party, Society, and Local Elite in the Jiangxi Communist Movement," *Journal of Asian Studies* 46, no. 2 (May 1987): 279.

17. As was then common among Communist organizers, Li called the base area government a "soviet." The official history of Poyang contains detailed discussions of the Pearl Lake (Zhuhu) Soviet. But one footnote admits that there is some doubt that the soviet was in fact formed; according to their investigation, it was "entirely possible" that the soviet existed, citing a history of party activity in the county as evidence. See *Poyang xian zhi*, 16.

18. For the discovery of the party branch headquarters, see ibid., 295.

19. His rise to county-chief would have been unimaginable in imperial times when magistrates were always outsiders. But during the Republic, especially in times of crisis, a local man such as Jiang could rise to considerable power over his hometown. The first magistrate to rule over Poyang County after the fall of the Qing, Zuo Xiangzhong, was a Poyang native. Zuo and Jiang Bozhang are the only Poyang natives to serve as county leaders during the Republic, but others hailed from Nanchang and other nearby places. See ibid., 424.

20. Jiang Bozhang was deputized as commander of the Second Region for this campaign. The Xiaolingshan base area was briefly re-established before getting crushed for a second time by forces under Jiang Bozhang, who then led the Security Regiment to "clear the countryside." According to Jiangxi historians, Jiang and his men murdered, burned, and looted their way through villages. See ibid., 17, 294.

21. The Red Tenth Army was first founded in the spring of 1929 as the North Jiangxi Northeast Independent Red Army (*Gan dongbei duli tuan*), becoming the Red Tenth Army in July 1930. After Jiang Bozhang oversaw the destruction of the Xiaojialing base area, the remnants of the Xiaojialing Guerrilla Band (1928–30) joined up with the Red Tenth Army. They broke through Jiang Bozhang's carefully established defensive lines and took the

high ground to the northwest of the town at Mount Zhi, capturing the cannons there. The city walls, never repaired after the Taipings captured the town eight decades earlier, had long ceased to offer much defense. The Red Tenth Army first seized the town on August 26. Before the month was over the Nationalists sent warships and airplanes from Nanchang in a surprise attack on Poyang Town; the Red Tenth Army quickly departed and returned to the countryside. They returned October 6 for a second short occupation. There was another moment of revolutionary activity in the countryside in 1933–34 with the brief formation of a base area in Zhihua Mountain (*Zhihuashan geming genjudi*). See ibid., 17.

22. Jiang Bozhang ran the dominant faction, linked to the powerful CC Clique. He had a worthy rival in Zhou Xiongyong, a Poyang Nationalist who rose to prominence working in government posts in Shanghai and Canton. Zhou's faction, while never able to outmaneuver Jiang Bozhang, had seized control over local financial institutions and was a force to be reckoned with. Ibid., 373.

23. There is very little evidence of how local governments functioned during these years. See ibid., 56.

24. For English-language accounts of the coming of the war: "Japanese Extend Range of Bombing. Many Cities, Railways, Aerodromes Attacked and Number of Chinese Planes Destroyed," *North-China Herald and Supreme Court and Consular Gazette*, December 22, 1937, 445; "Japan Bombs Imperil Americans. United States Warships Race to Swatow, South China Port, to Evacuate Nationals; 500 Killed and Wounded Toll of Air Raids," *Los Angeles Times*, July 3, 1938, 1; "Lake Is Reddened by Chinese Battle. Japanese Gain West Bank of Poyang in Week-Long Fight," *Atlanta Constitution*, July 25, 1938, 16.

25. Despite briefly taking Poyang Town in the summer of 1942, the Japanese left the county alone. Very little is known about Ding Guobing, the assassinated county-chief. According to Poyang historians, as county-chief he oversaw the destruction of local temples in 1942. Did a disgruntled believer get revenge? Had Jiang Bozhang's faction been involved in the assassination? Jiang himself was busy in Nanchang, where he had graduated from killing Communists to serving as a provincial senator. In his spare time, he even helped write the official history of the Nationalist Party. See *Poyang xian zhi*, 199, 373, 384.

26. To complicate matters, two different units of cadres played a role in the early administration of the county. The initial administration was controlled by cadres attached to the Second Field Army, with cadres from the Fourth Field Army taking over Poyang administration in late August 1949. See ibid., 20. Very few of them would have spoken Gan, one of ten major dialects of Chinese. As Mobo Gao notes, the Gan dialect can be further subdivided. The Gan Chinese of Poyang County is different from the Gan Chinese spoken in Nanchang. And even inside the county there are differences in the way locals

speak. Villagers, for example, have difficulty understanding the Gan Chinese spoken in Poyang Town. See Mobo C. F. Gao, *Gao Village: Modern Life in Rural China* (Honolulu: University of Hawaii Press, 1995), 10. The cadres assigned to Poyang were a fraction of a much larger force organized for the takeover of Nationalist-held regions. As discussed by James Gao, in 1948 the party had called for the training of some 53,000 cadres for this task, estimating that a county such as Poyang would need seventy-five cadres. Recruiting northern cadres to travel south was hampered by the localism of rural cadres, who preferred to return to farming once the Civil War ended. Southbound cadres were also forbidden from marriage for two years, lest they lose focus on the task at hand. To balance these factors, the party emphasized the honor of serving the revolution and gave southbound cadres a promotion. These cadres were not all farmers. Other southbound cadres included intellectuals, student activists, and former government employees. See James Gao, *The Communist Takeover of Hangzhou: The Transformation of City and Cadre, 1949–1954* (Honolulu: University of Hawaii Press, 2004), 19–52.

27. *Poyang xian zhi*, 736–39, 924.

28. Ibid., 532.

29. Southbound cadres initially preserved the Nationalist government structure, with separate town and county governments, but quickly moved to fold the town administration into the county government. When the first modern style county government is set up in 1926, public security (*gong'an*) was one of four departments, along with finance, education, and construction. The Nationalist police system had gone through multiple administrative changes. Most important, the bureau had been renamed the Inspection Office (*jianchaju*) in 1937, and police stations (*jianchasuo*) were established in district governments. Each of the district governments established by the Nationalists also had a police force. As with most things in Poyang during the Republican Era, some of these plans may have only existed on paper. Ibid., 420, 506.

30. As a result, locals had a saying that declared "where there is Public Security, no one is secure." Edward Friedman, Paul G. Pickowicz, and Mark Selden, *Chinese Village, Socialist State* (New Haven, CT: Yale University Press, 1993), 153.

31. The southbound cadres originally set up dual public security bureaus for the county and city, but the city administration was eventually folded into the county government. As of 1950 the Public Security Bureau had three sections: administration, political, and public security. They also oversaw detention centers and a Public Security Squadron (*gong'an dui*). See *Poyang xian zhi*, 507.

32. For street-name changes, see *Poyang xian zhi*, 65. For commercial traffic, see *Renmin ribao* [The people's daily], June 23, 1949, 1.

33. This poetic description of Poyang farming, courtesy of Mobo Gao, refers to the county's more recent history. As Mobo Gao said of the residents of

Poyang's Gao Village, no one had "experienced any war and nobody has ever died in battle." Villagers heard about the long-haired Taiping rebels but never saw one. And while the Japanese had briefly occupied Poyang Town, they had not ventured into the countryside. Gao, *Gao Village*, 5–7, 31.

34. For an overview of local agriculture see *Poyang xian zhi*, 561–64; for rural housing, see 746. Jiangxi counties shipped their surplus rice down the Yangtze to wealthier provinces in the Jiangnan region. See Philip Huang, *The Peasant Family and Rural Development in the Yangzi Delta, 1350–1988* (Stanford, CA: Stanford University Press, 1990), 123. For more on farming see Gao, *Gao Village*, 32, 59, 7–9.

35. Bamboo rods are used to construct the frames for the nets used by local fishermen. And bamboo is used to make two essential tools for rice farming: "the baskets used on shoulder poles to carry rice from the field, and a sort of mattress on which rice is dried." For bamboo nets, see R. Cunningham, "When the Bamboo Flowers," *North-China Herald and Supreme Court and Consular Gazette*, September 30, 1916, 691. For bamboo farming tools, see Gao, *Gao Village*, 227. For more on the county's forests see *Poyang xian zhi*, 588. Unsaid in the county gazetteer is the deforestation that occurred during the second half of the twentieth century. Gao notes that demand for firewood during these years significantly reduced Poyang forests. Now that firewood is no longer required for cooking, however, Poyang trees are making a comeback. Gao, *Gao Village Revisited*, 71–72. Gao also explains the connections between forestry and filial piety: "the better and thicker the timber and the heavier the coffin, the more filial the offspring and hence more honored and respected the family is in the eyes of the villagers." Gao, *Gao Village*, 230.

36. In Chinese: "*Jiefangjun you qianjunwanma, wo you qian shan wan ling.*" *Jiangxi sheng gongan shi: 1949–1959* [Jiangxi Province public security history, 1949–1959] (Nanchang: Jiangxi sheng gongan ting, 1994), 240, 292.

37. For the flood, see "Rising Yangtze Threatens Greatest Flood Since '31," *New York Times*, July 11, 1949, 8; *Poyang xian zhi*, 139. The commander of the attack on Poyang Town, named Ye Fen, was said to be part of the Ninth Route Army, but he may have simply been an outlaw searching for guns. As a result of his attack on Poyang Town, county leaders were forced to move their offices. See *Poyang xian zhi*, 20.

38. *Jiangxi sheng gongan shi*, 4–5.

39. The ambush on the grain barges took place at Lake Chihu, northwest of Lake Poyang. *Poyang xian zhi*, 20.

40. It is unclear how many were locals, but 1,012 were new recruits. *Jiangxi sheng gongan shi*, 7.

41. Citing the lake's ample commercial traffic and nearby mountain lairs, the Communists identified Lake Poyang as a high-priority target for bandit suppression. *Jiangxi sheng gongan shi*, 293.

42. The campaigns eliminated over 40,000 bandits, who possessed some

900,000 rifles and pistols, and another 2,000 machine guns. For an overview of these campaigns, see *Jiangxi sheng gongan shi*, 294–96.

43. The Second Field Army, led by Commander Liu Bocheng and political commissar Deng Xiaoping, met considerable resistance in the southwest. See Brown, 109.

44. For an overview of early party and government organizational schemes, see *Poyang xian zhi*, 491.

45. Ibid., 21.

46. Gao, *Gao Village*, 96.

47. *Renmin ribao*, May 8, 1950, 2, and June 11, 1950, 2.

48. For electricity see *Poyang xian zhi*, 736–39. Some Poyang villages had electricity by the late 1950s, but others had to wait until the 1980s. And even after the arrival of electricity there was "always a shortage of electricity." Gao, *Gao Village Revisited*, 121. Movies were first projected at the theater in 1951. Movie projection teams were sent to the countryside starting in 1955. *Poyang xian zhi*, 921. For teahouses in Poyang see *Poyang xian zhi*, 759. For a detailed discussion of teahouses in the People's Republic, see Di Wang, *The Teahouse under Socialism: The Decline and Renewal of Public Life in Chengdu, 1959–2000* (Ithaca, NY: Cornell University Press, 2018).

49. Government employees also received very limited spending money as needed. *Poyang xian zhi*, 491–92; 507.

50. For more on the Judicial Administrative Section (*sifa ke*) see *Poyang xian zhi*, 445–46.

51. Approved on September 29, 1949, the Common Program (*gongtong gangling*) was the law of the land during the first years of the new regime. It was replaced by a formal constitution in 1954.

52. For more on the People's Court (*fayuan*) and the People's Tribunal (*renmin fating*) see Liu Shigu, "'Shixu' xia de 'zhixu': xin Zhongguo chengli chuqi tugai zhong de sifa Shijian—dui Poyang xian 'bufa dizhu an' de jiedu yu fenxi" ["Order" under "disorder": Judicial practice during New China establishment initial period land reform—An interpretation and analysis of "illegal landlord cases" in Poyang County], *Jinshidai yanjiu* [Contemporary history research] 6 (2015): 93–96.

53. Li Kwok-sing, *A Glossary of Political Terms of the People's Republic of China*, translated by Mary Lok (Hong Kong: The Chinese University of Hong Kong Press, 1995), 457.

54. *Neibu cankao* [Internal reference materials] (Beijing: Xinhua chuban-she, November 9, 1950), 31–33.

55. The new regime executed 710,000 citizens during this movement. Another 1,290,000 were locked up, and 1,230,000 were put under surveillance. Li Kwok-sing, *Glossary of Political Terms*, 567. For more on this campaign see Julia Strauss, "Paternalist Terror: The Campaign to Suppress Counterrevolutionaries and Regime Consolidation in the People's Republic of China, 1950–1953," *Society for Comparative Study of Society and History* 44, no. 1 (2002): 80–105.

56. For spies in Fujian see *Neibu cankao* (August 17, 1950), 49–50; for bandits in Hunan see *Neibu cankao* (October 19, 1950), 143–45; for secret cabals see *Neibu cankao* (December 6, 1950), 29; for bandits in Guilin see *Neibu cankao* (October 12, 1950), 91; for bandits in Guangxi see *Neibu cankao* (November 28, 1950), 143–45.

Casefile 1: Bandits, Big Swords, and the Rebel Scholar

1. These mountains had long sheltered bandit gangs, including one led by the notorious Hemp-Skin Cao. Eastern Mountain Ridge (Dongshanlong) is now a community in Xiejiatan District, Shimenjie Township.

2. Nothing is known about any of these men outside of the files from this investigation, but the man Frightened Shi sought out shared a surname and a character from his given name with one of the bandit chiefs, suggesting the two men were closely related. I have chosen to obscure Frightened Shi's actual name, as well as the majority of the names discovered in the casefiles, to protect the identities of the citizens involved in the four investigations. I have opted, however, to provide the true names of the individuals who were well known enough to appear in *Poyang xian zhi*. For this casefile: Zhu Baihua, Xie Dongsheng, and Wang Zhenhai.

3. This chapter is based on "Materials on Poyang County, Northern Poyang Spies, Bandits, and Secret Society Activity" (*Poyang xian Pobei tewu tufei huimen huodong cailiao*), casefile Z2-1-52 from the Poyang County Public Security Bureau. At sixty-three pages, it is by far the longest of the four casefiles used in this book. The case was compiled by the Internal Political Cleansing Leading Small Group Office (*Neibu zhengzhi qingli lingdaozu bangongshi*); the stationary used for the case's cover page is from the 1960s, leading me to believe that this case was archived between the Great Leap Forward and the Cultural Revolution. Like all the casefiles used in this book, this one contains multiple documents, most of which lack clear authors, dates, and titles. This casefile includes multiple overviews of the crimes in question, "criminal reflection material" (*fanren fanxing cailiao*), and various court documents. Because much of the information of the case is jumbled and scattered through the files, citing every reference to the documents would render this book unreadable. For this reason, only direct quotes and points of interest are cited. For an overview of similar documents, see Liu Shigu, "Using Local Public Security Archives from the 1950s—Poyang County, Jiangxi," in *Fieldwork in Modern Chinese History: A Research Guide*, ed. Thomas David DuBois and Jan Keily (New York: Routledge, 2020), 282–88. Liu recounts how the History Department of Shanghai Jiaotong University obtained these files. As Liu explains, the Poyang County government had asked the department for help with a genealogy website. Historians, chatting with a local scholar over dinner, inquired about document collections. This led to the discovery of a treasure trove of Public Security Bureau files, stacked up and collecting dust. After obtaining permission from local authorities, researchers spent three

years digitizing the cases. Professor Cao Shuji oversaw the project, a massive effort that required researchers working eight to ten hours a day through hot summers and freezing winters. According to Liu, there are over 9,000 cases. While the discovery of this archive was a happy accident, I am also grateful that this archive existed in the first place. As Michael Schoenhals has discussed in his study of the Public Security Bureau, many rural offices didn't see the value of compiling an archive. In 1958, to cite one of his examples, the official bureau journal reminded local officers just how useful a well-run archive could be for their purposes. In the article, a township party secretary is quoted as saying that "a public security archive is a substantial resource in the struggle against the adversary and should be valued accordingly." Another article noted how the archive gave public security officers instant access to information about suspect elements within the local community. According to Schoenhals, in 1960 the value of these archives "exempted them from the rule that the contents of closed files . . . be automatically transferred to the corresponding state district, municipal, or provincial archive after a fixed period of time." See Michael Schoenhals, *Spying for the People: Mao's Secret Agents, 1949–1967* (Cambridge: Cambridge University Press, 2013), 129–32.

4. William Rowe, *China's Last Empire: The Great Qing* (Cambridge, MA: Belknap Press, 2012), 176.

5. "Soldiers Set Out to Save Captured Hanyang Priest. 2,500 troops Seek Trace of Rev. Lalor in Wuhan Area," *China Press*, May 24, 1928, 18. During these years, the Nationalists referred to Communist guerrilla units as "bandits," and the Western press was quick to adopt their rhetoric. See "Bandits Feared at Poyang. Sporadic Attacks by Communist Marauders," *North-China Herald and Supreme Court and Consular Gazette*, March 1, 1933, 332.

6. *Poyang xian zhi*, 508.

7. These events were originally dated in the old lunar calendar. The location for given for the attack is the Poyang's Fifth District, although the events discussed here occurred before the new county government established its district system.

8. The leader of the Communist garrison, named in the casefile, doesn't appear in the list of martyrs in the county gazetteer, which focuses on local martyrs. A People's Liberation Army propagandist from Poyang Town is listed as being martyred in Xiejiatan in July 1949. See *Poyang xian zhi*, 334. When and even if reinforcements ever arrived is one of many details left out of the archives. In his confession, Golden Cao made sure to emphasize that he was not a leader among the bandits in the Eastern Ridge Mountains. Z2–1-52, 13.

9. Rowe, *China's Last Empire*, 177.

10. These men were in the Gelaohui. "Notes from the Native Papers: Shenpao," *North-China Herald and Supreme Court and Consular Gazette*, July 15, 1892, 98.

11. Wang Di, *Violence and Order on the Chengdu Plain: The Story of a*

Secret Brotherhood in Rural China, 1939–1949 (Stanford, CA: Stanford University Press, 2018), 2; Rowe, *China's Last Empire*, 178–79.

12. These early Big Swords were a force for order, helping Qing officials suppress bandits. But with success grew danger. Once the Big Swords had recruited over 100,000 men in Shandong, the society began to seem rather dangerous to local Qing officials. After the Big Swords clashed with Catholics and endangered the Qing's fragile peace with imperialist powers, they had to go. Invited to the yamen to meet with Qing officials, Big Sword leaders walked into a trap. Once they were decapitated, the Big Swords of Shandong were no more. Esherick notes that he found a mysterious mention of a Big Sword Society in Northern Anhui in 1735 but was not able to make any connections between Anhui and Shandong. See Joseph W. Esherick, *The Origins of the Boxer Uprising* (Berkeley: University of California Press, 1987), 96–119. The relationship between the Big Swords of Shandong and Poyang are, unsurprisingly given the nature of the organization, decidedly mysterious. Shandong locals revived the Big Swords to fight Japanese invaders. Another Big Sword Society popped up further south in Jiangsu during the 1930s, again in self-defense. This time the Big Swords were organized to fight off a rival secret society, the Small Swords. At this point the Communists, fighting for their lives, fully embraced the Big Swords as potential allies: in 1940, 43% of Big Swords in Anhui enlisted in the Communists' New Fourth Army. See Elizabeth J. Perry, *Rebels and Revolutionaries in North China, 1845–1945* (Stanford, CA: Stanford University Press, 1980), 171–72, 229. From Anhui, Big Sword organization seems to have spread south to Jiangxi, which had its own history of martial arts practices. In 1875 the Western press, reporting an insurrection in Poyang, noted that most of those involved were farmers, led by those skilled in martial arts. "Abstract of Peking Gazettes," *North-China Herald and Supreme Court and Consular Gazette*, January 14, 1875, 27.

13. Li Kwok-sing, *A Glossary of Political Terms*, 85–86.

14. The Big Swords are said to have organized 190 branches, 380 leaders, and over 4,000 members. According to Poyang historians, the Big Swords were taken over by Nationalist spies. *Poyang xian zhi*, 509.

15. Hengyong Township was one of thirty-six township administrations in the Republic of China. The township oversaw 10 administrative hamlets (*bao*), 104 administrative neighborhoods (*jia*), and 78 natural villages (*zirancun*). *Poyang xian zhi*, 56. The township government office (*xiang gongsuo*) was almost certainly located alongside Hengyong Dam, but the whole place is underwater now, buried beneath the Junmin Water Reservoir. First imagined by Houjiagang Commune cadres during the Great Leap Forward, the reservoir was constructed in the early 1970s. I only discovered this after spending many hours searching for Hengyong. To further complicate matters, this place might have been pronounced "Hengchong."

16. I have chosen this translation instead of the original, which ends: "even Su Wu cannot surpass him." Su Wu was a model of courage and faithful ser-

vice from the Han dynasty. *Poyang xian zhi*, 274. Researching this thread, I discovered that Hong's personal library counted 10,000 volumes. Given the academic success of his sons, I heartily endorse building more libraries. See Joseph P. McDermott, "Book Collecting in Jiangxi," in *Knowledge and Text Production in an Age of Print—China, 900–1400*, ed. Lucille Chia and Hilde De Weerdt (Leiden: Brill, 2011), 98.

17. The exam system was interrupted at the end of the imperial era. At the dawn of the twentieth century, Lake Poyang became a hotbed for anti-Western sentiment. On a hill not far from the lake, missionaries erected a cross to commemorate the recent crucifixion of a Catholic priest. The Qing dynasty, desperate to quell anti-foreign protest in the aftermath of the Boxer Uprising, took note, canceling Poyang County examinations for five years as punishment. "Imperial Decrees," *North-China Herald and Supreme Court and Consular Gazette*, June 19, 1901, 1188.

18. He had engraved four characters on his sword: *zhongyi baoguo*. *Poyang xian zhi*, 284.

19. Various states had taken an interest in promoting education, but little progress had been made. Among a flurry of late Qing reforms, the dynasty established an Educational Promotional Bureau and a county library. The bureau died with the dynasty, and in a few years the library's collection was lost. The Nationalist regime pushed for the establishment of elementary schools throughout the county, calling for the establishment of a central elementary school at the township level, with elementary schools at the hamlet level. But in the final months before the dawn of New China, the county's informal network of private academies, 753 strong, was still Poyang's primary educational force. *Poyang xian zhi*, 957–58. This conflation of township and "united hamlet" is a bit of a simplification. This administrative system was originally the *baolian* system, first created in 1931. The "united hamlet" (*baolian*) was later changed to township (*xiang*).

20. Four years after he started school, Scholarly Wu began studying under his Uncle Wang from his mother's family, only to have this uncle die two years later. In his late teens he studied under his last teacher, a Confucian scholar who decades ago had some success in the exam system. For more on rural education see Gao, *Gao Village*, 15; *Poyang xian zhi*, 966.

21. The dates for events here and throughout have been converted from the lunar calendar. In his confessions, Scholarly Wu twice notes that Boss Wang called the hamlet-chiefs (*baozhang*) of the township to the meeting. This would suggest that there was a clear connection, if not a considerable overlap, between administrative leadership and the Big Swords. Or perhaps he was simply using the language of the state in his confession.

22. The People's Liberation Army didn't suppress the Guizhou rebels until 1951. Jeremy Brown describes this resistance as "shockingly successful." See Jeremy Brown, "From Resisting Communists to Resisting America: Civil War and Korean War in Southwest China, 1950–1951," in *Dilemmas of Victory:*

The Early Years of the People's Republic of China, ed. Jeremy Brown and Paul. G. Pickowicz (Cambridge, MA: Harvard University Press, 2007), 105.

23. Huangtugang in the documents, now called Huangtupo. Throughout the casefile, security officers refer to localities through a numerical administration system; this hamlet is described as Hengyong's 5th *bao*. The casefile mentions ten hamlets, and according to Poyang historians there were in fact ten hamlets in Hengyong Township. *Poyang xian zhi*, 56.

24. He was also accompanied by a man from the Wu clan on this walk.

25. Edward L. Davis, *Society and the Supernatural in Song China* (Honolulu: University of Hawaii Press, 2001), 52.

26. There is no mention of this *zijiujun* in *Poyang xian zhi*.

27. Scholarly Wu really spilled his guts here, naming a half dozen Big Swords as the ones responsible for the deaths. Z2–1-52, 15.

28. Why he would use the phrase *dadaohui ye jiefang le* is one of the many questions unanswered in the casefile. Note that while Scholarly Wu and General Hong did make co-confessions, in this solo confession Scholarly Wu emphasizes the crimes of General Hong. Z2–1-52, 15.

29. Another "bandit-general," surnamed Yang, played a smaller role in the events described in this section. The date of the ambush is confirmed by one of the rare published mentions of Pig Mouth Mountain, which also notes the date of this attack. According to that sparse account, over 400 Big Swords from Chuanwan Township ambushed soldiers sent from Fuliang to suppress bandits. "'Jiulujun' de fumie" [The destruction of the "Ninth Route Army"], in *Qing jiao fei te de gushi* [Stories of eliminating bandits and spies], ed. Li Qingshan (Beijing: Zhonggong dangshi chubanshe, 2004), 119.

30. The documents refer to Chuanwan, a community in the mountains of northern Poyang, in three ways: as a village (*cun*), a township (*xiang*), and a district (*qu*). The confusion is most likely a byproduct of the shifting administrative systems as the Nationalist order was replaced by the Communists' new regime. Chuanwan had been the site of a Nationalist township government, and the Communists most likely had taken over this office. This office, as luck would have it, is one of the rare township governments that Poyang historians discuss: Communist sympathizers worked through the Chuanwan township office (Chuanwan *xiang gongsuo*) to carry out anti-Japanese propaganda during the early 1940s. See *Poyang xian zhi*, 338. Despite repeated references in the documents to a district government (*qu zhengfu*), according to Poyang historians there was never a district government established in Chuanwan. But perhaps authors using the character for "district" (*qu*) were using it in a broader sense of "region" or "area."

31. The casefile contains conflicting reports as to the exact number of weapons involved in this attack. The bandits were armed with an assortment of rifles and pistols and may have had a crossbow and an artillery tube as well.

32. Xu's men came from three hamlets: the 1st, 2nd, and 3rd *bao*.

33. Fiery Huang's power base was in the township's 6th and 7th *bao*. Just how many Big Swords he had with him varies from document to document.

34. The column was made up of men from three of the eight hamlets under Boss Wang's personal control. These are referred to as the 8th, 9th, and 10th *bao*. In one account Scholarly Wu also gets the 7th, but this goes unmentioned in his own account of the attack.

35. This is a bit of a simplification. Boss Wang's men were said to be heading to Houjiagang, a market town, to meet up with Xie Old Seven, but it is unclear if they intended to meet at the actual town or in the general area.

36. These men came from the five other hamlets under his control: the 1st, 2nd, 3rd, 4th, and 5th *bao*.

37. Old Seven served as the "head commander" of the assault. Z2–1-52, 26.

38. *Jiangxi sheng gongan shi*, 291.

39. The bandits were armed with fourteen rifles, eight pistols, and an artillery shell tube.

40. Z2–1-52, 8.

41. Public Security Bureau reports never clarified how many Chuanwan Big Swords came out that day, in contrast to well-documented account of the Hengyong Big Swords.

42. The list of martyrs compiled by county historians names one Poyang man, Zhou Caifa of Youcheng, who was killed in action in June, 1949 in Chuanwan. *Poyang xian zhi*, 328.

43. They used the local term for gods: bodhisattvas. Z2–1-52, 7.

44. As the officer noted: *yunyong tufei shouwan gaomiao*. Z2–1-52, 31.

45. The last word on him comes from a joint confession; he is said to have gone to Zhide County, which is an alternate name for Dongzhi County, his hometown in Anhui. Z2–1-52, 8.

46. Of the bandit leaders who had scared him into handing over a bribe of produce, most had been eventually caught in neighboring Fuliang. Only one, from the Wang family, remained on the run. Z2–1-52, 13.

47. It is unclear if they three were captured or turned themselves in. The three prisoners collaborated to explain the events of the crimes in question to Poyang security officers. For example, the three worked together (*tong zhi*) to produce an overview of the events and those involved: Z2–1-52, 7. Poyang security officers would have the men produce new documents to further explain events as needed, including a supplementary report dated July 16, 1950: Z2–1-52, 8.

48. Like Big Tiger in the next chapter, Scholarly Wu made sure to note that he had been a "fake" government official. He admitted to embezzling

grain during his brief stint as township-chief. The county-chief in question was Ding Guobing (assassinated in 1944), but in the document in question the name is written incorrectly as Ding Guowei. This is just one of the many errors found in the casefiles.

49. Z2–1-52, 14.

50. This prison, first established in the late Qing on what the Communists now called May 1st Avenue (then Heng Jie), had twenty-two cells, two of which were reserved for women prisoners. Except for two temporary rural jails, established in 1930 during the Communists' brief revolutionary upswing, the Nationalist had no infrastructure for imprisoning villagers. For more on Poyang prisons, see *Poyang xian zhi*, 519.

51. He was first detained by the 481st Regiment. At the time of this confession, in which Scholarly Wu details his path through various lockups, Scholarly Wu had been incarcerated for 204 days in three prisons. Most of that time, 183 days, had been in Poyang, but according to his confession Scholarly Wu had only been laboring in the prison camp (called a "factory") for a little over a month. It is unclear where else he was imprisoned while he was in Poyang. Z2–1-52, 14. Scholarly Wu entered prison camp well before the system was regularized in Jiangxi and Poyang. According to local gazetteers, it was not until the summer of 1951 that the province established reform through labor production units (*laogai shengchan danwei*) for reform through education, including farms (*nongchang*); this followed an August 25, 1950 provincial directive, calling on prison administrators working in the Public Security Bureau to emphasize education. *Jiangxi sheng sifa xingzheng zhi* [Jiangxi province judicial administration gazetteer] (Jiangxi renmin chubanshe, 1995), 131–33.

52. The three wrote a joint confession, most likely penned by Scholarly Wu, on July 16, 1950. Z2–1-52, 26.

53. Philip F. Williams and Yenna Wu, *The Great Wall of Confinement: The Chinese Prison Camp through Contemporary Fiction and Reportage* (Berkeley: University of California Press, 2004), 52–55.

54. Administratively, the camp was under the county detention center. The name changed (in July 1950) from Poyang xinsheng gongchang to Poyang xian gong'anju laodong gaizao dui. At that time the camp housed fifty-eight criminals, divided into six small production units. *Poyang xian zhi*, 519.

55. Ibid., 14.

56. The location of their capture was Huangtupo Village, right where Boss Wang called the second meeting. Ibid., 508.

57. For an example of the men being call "bandit spies" (*fei te*): Z2–1-52, 8.

58. *Poyang xian zhi*, 508.

Casefile 2: Big Tiger, Tyrant of the Mountain

1. Comrade Zhou joined the Anhui-Zhejiang-Jiangxi Detachment (Wan Zhe Gan zhidui), Northern Jiangxi Guerrilla Warfare Military Command Center (Ganbei youji silingbu). He carried out aide-de-camp work (*fuguan gongzuo*). This account is based on casefile Z1–3-329, labeled with the name of the accused. This casefile, containing thirty-three pages, is significantly smaller than the collection of documents used for casefile 1. The documents inside the casefile, however, are generally in much better condition. Because this case went to trial at the People's Tribunal, it offers our first look into the legal system the Communists installed in Poyang. According to its cover page, the casefile was archived by the Poyang County Politics and Law Office (Zhengfa bangongshi), which was established in 1958. Personal names taken from the casefile in question have been changed, except for the well-known Jiang Beiran, who of course appears in *Poyang xian zhi.*

2. Comrade Hou is the stubborn cipher of this story. The documents tell two conflicting stories about this man, and in fact use two different names. In one, told by Comrade Zhou's son, he was a security officer working to bring revolution to the countryside (*jingwei ying jipao lian zhong shi*; guard battalion machine cannon company middle soldier). Most of the documents give the man a slightly different given name and portray him as nothing more than an innocent bystander, a traveling merchant from Duchang who was in the wrong place at the wrong time. For an example of Hou as an innocent businessman in a report compiled by the township, see Z1–3-329, 8; for Hou as a security officer, Z1–3-329, 10. In the end, because all agree that Hou was, like Comrade Zhou, from Duchang, I have decided to trust the minority opinion of Comrade Zhou's son. It seems much more logical that he was there as a security officer rather than a businessman. I have also considered the possibility that there were in fact two related men; that would explain the similar names. But not a single document raised the idea of there being three victims in the attack. Sadly, none of these names appear in the list of revolutionary martyrs in the Duchang County gazetteer. See *Duchang xian zhi* (Beijing: Xinhua chubanshe, 1992), 560.

3. According to Filial Zhou, Dayuan was the Thirteenth Hamlet in the Jiantian Township. The documents note this part of Poyang as belonging to the Second District, headquartered in Tianfan Street. But oddly, multiple documents refer to this as the 9th District; that district was based in Sanmiaoqian, far to the south near Poyang Town. The documents offer no clue to these discrepancies. Nowadays Dayuan Village sits next to the Dayuan River Reservoir, built during the Great Leap Forward. Dayuan Village escaped the fate of Hengyong, one of the key locations in casefile 1, which was destroyed by its reservoir. Finding this village was greatly complicated by the fact that the documents typically referred to it using incorrect, but easier to write, characters.

4. This was the local hamlet-chief (*baozhang*) for the Thirteenth Ham-

let, which included Dayuan and Fengtian villages. He seems to have gotten the post sometime after the previous hamlet-chief, a landlord from the Huang clan, fled. The exact relationship between the hamlet (*bao*) and its neighborhoods (*jia*) in this corner of the county is unclear.

5. In 1949 there were only six local party branches in the county. In 1950 there were only fifteen local party branches, but by 1954 Poyang boasted 291 party branches in the county, with 256 of them in villages. During these first years Poyang Communists were a young group: more than half of them were under twenty-five years old, and not even one of them had more than a middle school education. *Poyang xian zhi*, 350–52.

6. Shi Nai-an and Luo Guanzhong, *Outlaws of the Marsh*, translated by Sidney Shapiro (Bloomington: Indiana University Press, 1981), 118.

7. Dates here and throughout are converted from the original lunar calendar dates.

8. The exact figure is 89.08%. *Poyang xian zhi*, 159.

9. Z1-3-329, 17.

10. A bit of a simplification: There were thirty-seven townships (*xiang*) and towns (*zhen*). Initially townships were called "united hamlets" (*bao-lian*). *Poyang xian zhi*, 516.

11. For a detailed examination of the breakdown of the *baojia* system in the late Qing, see Huaiyin Li, *Village Governance in North China: 1875–1936* (Stanford, CA: Stanford University Press, 2005), 42–46. As Li makes clear, the *baojia* system showed a high degree of regional variation. Li is focused on the *baojia* system in North China, but its tendency to devolve from its administrative ideal seems universal.

12. Philip Huang, *The Peasant Family and Rural Development in the Yangzi Delta, 1350–1988* (Stanford, CA: Stanford University Press, 1990), 38.

13. There was, to be sure, much variation in local tax collection procedures both temporally and geographically. Reed, 178–79.

14. Serving as the local *jia* leader carried risk as well as opportunity for profit. Many men avoided the task, especially when part of the job was finding conscripts for the Nationalist army. This often meant sending a member of your own lineage to war. In one small Poyang village, the unlucky man forced by his neighbors to serve as *jia* head, desperate to find a replacement conscript for his village, went bankrupt trying to pay off someone to enlist. Gao, *Gao Village*, 224–25.

15. The Jinghu roadway (*Jinghu gonglu*) goes between Lake Poyang at Hukou and Jingdezhen; this old road has long been replaced by a modern highway. The road was first built in the late 1920s and completed in 1937. It was partially destroyed to hinder the advance of Japanese forces. See *Poyang xian zhi*, 710.

16. The paper gave an account of seven Poyang women who died due

to domestic violence. Two were killed, five committed suicide. *Renmin ribao*, September 22, 1950, 3.

17. Gao, *Gao Village*, 224.

18. The documents do not make clear how closely related the two men were, beyond sharing the surname Li.

19. The documents refer to the secret society with two names. At times it is the Yellow Crane Society (Huanghe hui). At other times it is referred to as the Huang-Li Society (Huang Li hui). There is no evidence that the group practiced any martial arts training. As discussed in the following casefile, secret societies such as this one may have largely existed in the imaginations of security officers.

20. Z1-3-329, 13, 16, 19, 27.

21. He became the adopted son of a man from the Huang clan. His position in the secret society was a "schoolmaster" (*xuezhang*).

22. This Huang man was later described as a hardened bandit by officers. The documents list the names of most of the attackers. All but one is from the Li or Huang families.

23. A host of local officials were involved in mediating a settlement in the aftermath of the attack. According to Big Tiger's last confession, well after the events in question, he lists the mediators as Director Jiang, Political Commissar Leng, and hamlet-chief Wang. These are the only time they are mentioned in the documents. Z1-3-329, 5–6.

24. *Jiangxi sheng gongan shi*, 8–9.

25. Xi Zhongxun, "Guanyu tugai zhong yixie wenti gei Mao zhuxi de baogao" [A report to Chairman Mao concerning some problems in land reform], in *Zhongguo tudi gaige shiliao xuanbian* [Selected historical materials from China's land reform] (Beijing: Guofang daxue chubanshe, 1988), 451.

26. Liu Shigu, "'Shixu' xia de 'zhixu': xin Zhongguo chengli chuqi tugai zhong de sifa Shijian—dui Poyang xian 'bufa dizhu an' de jiedu yu fenxi" ["Order" under "disorder": Judicial practice during New China establishment initial period land reform—An interpretation and analysis of "illegal landlord cases" in Poyang County], *Jinshidai yanjiu* [Contemporary history research] 6 (2015): 93.

27. Filial Zhou links Big Tiger with the "fake National Salvation Militia" (*wei Jiuguotuan*), organized by Li Fengchun. This military force, also known as the Ninth Route Army, is discussed in casefile 4. Besides this claim by Filial Zhou, there is no evidence that links Big Tiger with the forces of Li Fengchun. Nor is there any evidence that Big Tiger was a member of the Big Sword Society.

28. Z1-3-329, 9–10.

29. This is one interpretation to his reference to a brawl (*oudou*) between the People's Government and fake township soldiers (*wei xiang bing*). There are no other references to this incident in the documents,

but I suspect there were physical altercations between Big Tiger and those who were attempting to bring him to justice. Z1-3-329, 17.

30. This was midway through Poyang's land reform campaigns, but the documents barely mention land reform. The archival documents are silent as to exactly where Big Tiger sat while in lock up. But in February 1950, the provincial government had decreed that evil tyrants such as Big Tiger, who had committed serious crimes, were to be arrested by county authorities and handled by the People's Tribunal. *Jiangxi sheng gongan shi*, 7.

31. These centers (*kanshousuo*) were typically run by the local Public Security Bureau or by branches of the People's Tribunal. *Jiangxi sheng sifa xingzheng zhi*, 131-33.

32. This ambush took place on June 9, 1950. The attackers made off with two rifles and a Mauser. *Jiangxi sheng gongan shi*, 9.

33. In this document, a confession in the form of a "self-reflection letter" (*fanxing shu*), Fengtian Village is listed as the 12th village of Jiantian Township. Z1-3-329, 17.

34. Ibid., 16.

35. Deng Zihui, "Cong Eqian xiang douzheng lai yanjiu muqian tudigaige yundong" [From Eqian Township struggle to researching current land reform movement], in *Zhongguo tudi gaige shiliao xuanbian* [Selected historical materials from China's land reform] (Beijing: Guofang daxue chubanshe, 1988), 293-94.

36. Confiscation of rich peasant property was officially approved with the Outline Land Law, released on October 10, 1947. More lenient treatment of rich peasants became official with the promulgation of the Land Reform Law of the People's Republic of China in the summer of 1950. Bo Yibo, *Ruogan zhongda juece yu shijian de huigu* [Recollections on some major policy decisions and events] (Beijing: Zhonggong zhongyang dang xiao chubanshi, 1991), 118-23.

37. Z1-3-329, 18.

38. Ibid., 19.

39. Ibid., 20.

40. The Nationalist legal system in Jiangxi dated back to October 1927, when the Nationalists sent out orders from their new capital in Nanjing, calling for a system of provincial courts. That month Jiangxi established a provincial High Court (*gaodeng fayuan*) to handle both criminal and civil cases. Courts in cities and counties followed, with the Poyang County Court (*xian fayuan*) established in 1929. See *Jiangxi sheng fayuan zhi* [Jiangxi Province court gazetteer] (Fangzhi chuban she, 1996), 12-14. My understanding of Poyang's dual track legal system benefited greatly from Chenxi Luo, who presented her paper, "Who Is Counterrevolutionary? Understanding the Campaign to Suppress Counterrevolutionaries in the Early PRC from a Bifurcated Local Institution," at the 2020 AAS in Asia

Conference, held remotely from Kobe, Japan. In Jiangxi the new People's Court system started with a provincial court founded just months after the capital in Nanchang was liberated. First came the Jiangxi Provincial People's Court on July 1, 1949. That same day the Communists formally reorganized Nanchang Prison, which had previously been taken over by the People's Liberation Army; the prison accepted criminals from the provincial People's Court as well as local Nanchang prisoners. *Jiangxi sheng sifa xingzheng zhi*, 131–33. The following year saw courts established in cities, prefectures, and counties, including one in Poyang Town. In May 1950 counties, cities, and prefectures were ordered to create judicial administrative sections, leading to a surge in courts: by the end of the year, Jiangxi had seventy-eight people's courts. That same month a branch of the provincial court was established in Fuliang, overseeing seven county courts including one in Poyang. *Jiangxi sheng fayuan zhi*, 18–20.

41. Eighty-two tribunals were set up at the city or county level, while districts boasted over 400. *Jiangxi sheng fayuan zhi*, 22.

42. The branches were located at Forty Mile Street, Xiejiatan, Youdunjie, Houjiagang, Huanggang, Tianfanjie, Old County Crossing, and Sixiling. *Poyang xian zhi*, 445.

43. Five other individuals were listed as part of the conspiracy. The charges also implicated the Ninth Route Army, discussed further in casefile 4.

44. Philip Kuhn, *Soulstealers: The Chinese Sorcery Scare of 1768* (Cambridge, MA: Harvard University Press, 1992), 15.

45. The key moment in this process was the "Revised Code," released in 1910 by the Qing dynasty. See Williams and Wu, 30.

46. The accused were held in detention centers; once sentenced, they were sent to prison camps. Detention centers went by multiple names (*kanshou suo, juliu suo, shourong suo*). *Poyang xian zhi*, 519. Officer Shi did not date his interrogation of Big Tiger.

47. Williams and Wu, *The Great Wall of Confinement*, 67–70.

48. There were 22,274 arrested. *Jiangxi sheng gongan shi*, 16.

49. Z1-3-329, 12.

50. According to his biography, he was classified with a "third level disability" (*san deng jiaji canfei*). *Poyang xian zhi*, 306–7.

51. The county tribunal was recently established in 1951. For more see *Poyang xian zhi*, 20–21.

52. This was a "clearing up criminals small group." Among the five members on the small group was an Officer Wu, who would interrogate Big Tiger on April 26, 1952, shortly before his execution; this document from the small group is undated. At some point it was updated with two red characters (*qiangjue*), indicating that the request to shoot Big Tiger had been approved, if not carried out. Z1–3–329, 24.

53. Specifically, the county leaders reached out to the Jiangxi Province

Fuliang District Administrative Inspector Government Office (Jiangxi sheng Fuliang qu xingzheng ducha gongshu). Z1-3-329, 29.

54. Ibid., 25.

55. In his confession he used the term "rape" for his relationship with Ms. Zhao; this legal charge does not seem to match the relationship as it is otherwise described in the documents. The officer who took his confession, Officer Wu, was on the review board that added a note of explanation to Judge Jiang's verdict. Z1-3-329, 16.

56. He said this about himself and the Huang man who mobilized the other half of the assassination squad. Z1-3-329, 15.

57. I have these Li men as brothers due to their similar names, but they could have easily been fraternal cousins.

58. Z1-3-329, 3.

59. When he had time, he did cook for his son, otherwise, as was often the case, his mother lent a hand and looked after her grandson. Big Tiger's wife died in 1948, meaning he was carrying on his affair while she was still alive. Z1-3-329, 18.

60. *Poyang xian zhi*, 546.

61. As one fictional detective posited: "It is a capital mistake to theorize before one has data. Insensibly one begins to twist facts to suit theories, instead of theories to suit facts."

Casefile 3: The Case of the Bodhisattva Society

1. Runaway Xu turned himself in on Monday, July 9. He was said to be from the Fifth District, based in Xiejiatan, up in the northern part of the county where Frightened Shi bribed bandits. The documents for this case come from casefile Z2-3-21. In contrast to the other cases used for this book, these documents were all written by security officers. There are no confessions or recorded interrogations. The casefile, which erroneously spells Runaway Xu's name, is labeled "The Case of the Fake 'Peasant Association.'" During land reform, landlords and other village elites sometimes created what the Communists called "fake" peasant associations to run local affairs. The secret association in question does not neatly fit into the category of a "fake" peasant association. The archivist who filed the case was working at some remove from the crime, but it is impossible to say how far: the folder is undated but was most likely archived by the Politics and Law Office. All of the names found in this casefile have been changed to obscure the identities of those involved.

2. For reports of violence in Jiangxi land reform, see: *Neibu cankao*, January 13, 1951, 42–44; *Neibu cankao*, December 27, 1950, 159–60; and *Neibu cankao*, February 2, 1951, 2–3.

3. For more on the Political Defense Section (Zhengzhi baowei gu), see *Poyang xian zhi*, 522.

4. "100,000 Move on Chinese Bandits. Nanking Authorities Also Use Planes in Attack on Communists," *Courier-Journal*, November 3, 1930, 1.

5. The exact name found for Comrade Cheng in this casefile does not appear in the long list of revolutionary martyrs in *Poyang xian zhi*. This caused no shortage of confusion and doubt for me over the past few years. It seems, however, that the officer drafting the document in question got one of the characters for Comrade Cheng's given name wrong. Except for one character in his name, the martyr mentioned in the casefile is a perfect fit for Cheng Yangshan. I only made this connection during the final round of revisions for this book. I have no direct evidence that Kuang Rong'en lived in or around Likuang Village, but this seems a reasonable speculation given the events in the casefile and the account of Cheng's downfall in *Poyang xian zhi*. For Cheng's story, see *Poyang xian zhi*, 293.

6. The events discussed in this case bounce between two directly adjacent villages. To avoid confusion, I have chosen to use Likuang Village as the location for this case.

7. This man may have been a fraternal cousin, not a brother. Z2–3-21, 183.

8. During the war he had also graduated from a Hankou cadre training program. Z2–3-21, 205.

9. For village compacts (*xiang gui min yue*) see *Poyang xian zhi*, 193.

10. The documents compiled by the new regime for this case were written by security officers unconcerned with its appearance. As Mobo Gao notes, Poyang villagers used the term "bodhisattva" (*pusa*) to describe any type of statue, including statues of Mao Zedong. The "bodhisattva" of Gao Village was Wang Taigong (Great Grandfather Wang or Grand Wang Buddha). Gao, *Gao Village*, 228.

11. Wang, *Violence and Order on the Chengdu Plain*, 2; Rowe, *China's Last Empire*, 57.

12. Edward L. Davis, *Society and the Supernatural in Song China* (Honolulu: University of Hawaii Press, 2001), 149.

13. Richard Von Glahn, *The Sinister Way: The Divine and the Demonic in Chinese Religious Culture* (Berkeley: University of California Press, 2004), 67–68.

14. During test point land reform seventy work team members carried out land reform throughout the Eighth District. The county's land reform campaigns produced 4,879 landlord households, out of a total of 120,643 households. A little over 5% of Poyang residents belonged to landlord households. For an overview of Poyang land reform, see *Poyang xian zhi*, 558–59. A re-examination campaign running from April 1951 to March 1952 ensured correct redistribution of the land. See Gao, *Gao Village*, 16.

15. Liu Shigu, "'Shixu' xia de 'zhixu': xin Zhongguo chengli chuqi tugai zhong de sifa Shijian—dui Poyang xian 'bufa dizhu an' de jiedu yu fenxi" ["Order" under "disorder": Judicial practice during New China establish-

ment initial period land reform—An interpretation and analysis of "illegal landlord cases" in Poyang County], *Jinshidai yanjiu* [Contemporary history research] 6 (2015): 93–97.

16. Ibid., 99–100.

17. As Elizabeth Perry notes, policies implemented by the work team could quickly be reversed once the team left, necessitating return visits. See Elizabeth J. Perry, "Making Communism Work: Sinicizing a Soviet Governance Practice," *Comparative Studies in Society and History* 61, no. 3 (2019): 16.

18. *Jiangxi sheng gongan shi*, 6.

19. Williams and Wu, *The Great Wall of Confinement*, 139.

20. Multiple dates are given for the jailbreak in the casefile. One report has Landlord Zhao beaten to death by other landlord detainees. Z2–3-21, 204

21. The two escapees' journey from jail to Likuang Village is one of the most confusing parts of the casefile. One of the clearer accounts makes clear that they were not always on the run together but both men ended up in Likuang Village. Luyuan Village, where they fled first, is about six miles away from Likuang Village. Ibid., 231.

22. Ibid., 204.

23. Von Glahn, *The Sinister Way*, 68.

24. The connection between these men and the return of the Nationalist order is a play on their given names. Z2–3-21, 184.

25. Ibid., 200.

26. Ibid., 231.

27. Ibid., 184.

28. Ibid., 204.

29. The Communists were not the first to attempt to control local dramatic performances. Back in 1917, a lakeside village rioted against an order that had prohibited theater performances, forcing the local magistrate to flee. See "Notes from Kiangsi," *North-China Herald and Supreme Court and Consular Gazette*, February 3, 1917, 220. For my exploration of the party's intervention into the cultural scene, see Brian James DeMare, *Mao's Cultural Army: Drama Troupes in China's Rural Revolution* (Cambridge: Cambridge University Press, 2015).

30. For more on Cheng Ming, including his early life living in what was then called Raozhou, see Chen Ming, *Wo yu Ding Ling wushi nian* [My fifty years with Ding Ling] (Beijing: Zhongguo da baike quanshu chubanshe, 2010).

31. For Poyang drama, see *Poyang xian zhi*, 917–21.

32. For a painfully dull depiction of thought reform among college students see *Sixiang wenti* [Ideological problems] (Beijing: Sanlian shudian, 1950). This spoken drama brings revolutionary education to life, which makes it an awful bore. The types of courses depicted in the play followed the example of Yan'an rectification and foreshadowed the thought reform campaigns that were just around the corner for these intellectuals. Merlie

Goldman called this style of reeducation "one of the most ambitious attempts at human manipulation in history." Merlie Goldman, "The Party and the Intellectuals," in *The Cambridge History of China*, ed. Roderick MacFarquhar and John K. Fairbank (Cambridge: Cambridge University Press, 1987), 223. See also Aminda M. Smith, *Thought Reform and China's Dangerous Classes: Reeducation, Resistance, and the People* (Lanham, MD: Rowman and Littlefield, 2012).

33. Z2–3-21, 198.

34. Michael Schoenhals translates "*neixian*" as "penetrating agent." According to Schoenhals, this term refers "to men or women who were actually inside the operational target." A more literal translation would be "inside thread." See Michael Schoenhals, *Spying for the People: Mao's Secret Agents, 1949–1967* (Cambridge: Cambridge University Press, 2013), 69.

35. Cadets training at the Central People's Public Security Academy in Beijing in 1957 were instructed that "in ordinary rural village areas, work is to be carried out by relying on the masses, without any further deployment of agents." Quoted in ibid., 5–6.

36. Z2–3-21, 184.

37. The farm is directly adjacent to Taiyangbu, where Comrade Cheng was betrayed in 1930. It is only a fifteen-minute walk between the two spots. For information on the farm, see *Poyang xian zhi*, 519.

38. The militiamen were mobilized by the local government (*dangdi zhengfu*); this could be a district or township government. The farmhands are called "production comrades" in the documents. This attack seems highly unlikely given the relative strength of the Bodhisattva Society and the new regime. Far more likely, the officers included this in their report to reflect their belief in the counterrevolutionary nature of evil tyrants. Z2–3-21, 185.

39. Williams and Wu, *The Great Wall of Confinement*, 139.

40. As officers noted, many individuals mentioned in their reports were not originally part of the Bodhisattva Society, only becoming implicated after the jailbreak brought them into the world of the Kuang family.

41. Z2–3-21, 185.

42. Gao, *Gao Village*, 229.

43. *Poyang xian zhi*, 519.

44. In order to reduce the number of cadres needed to oversee prisoners, labor camps had been organized in a military model. Prisoners were grouped in units designed to self-supervise: brigades, squads, and groups. Cadres would lead brigades as brigade heads (*duizhang*) or political instructors (*zhidaoyuan*). Williams and Wu, *The Great Wall of Confinement*, 50–51.

Casefile 4: Merchant Zha Goes to Court

1. Of the 840 Poyang residents who ended up in Taiwan, some were wealthy or Nationalists, but many were rank-and-file soldiers. *Poyang xian zhi*, 358.

2. Li Fengchun established a full organizational structure for his Defense Department Youth National Salvation Army (Guofangbu qingnian jiuguo jun), including a formal headquarters and cadre department (*zhengzhibu*). According to one account, with allies in local secret societies factored in, Li Fengchun could claim some 28,300 men. *Poyang xian zhi*, 508. Chang Kuo-sin, who spent eight months in the PRC, reported a Ninth Route Army active in the Henan-Anhui-Hubei area. According to Chang, the Ninth Route Army marched with slogans that defied simple characterization. Yes, they wanted to "Capture Mao Zedong Alive." But they also declared "Down with Chiang Kai-shek." Chang Kuo-sin, *Eight Months Behind the Bamboo Curtain: A Report on the First Eight Months of Communist Rule in China* (Hong Kong: City University Hong Kong Press, 2016), 76.

3. Readers will recall an earlier attack in Xiejiatan, discussed in casefile 1. The relationship between these two attacks remains unclear.

4. Zhou Huamin was the district party committee secretary (*qu wei shuji*). After land reform the county government constructed memorials commemorating Zhou Huamin and Guo Xue in Xiejiatan. They also named two local schools after Zhou Huamin and renamed a nearby village Guo Xue Village. At their memorial the party declared the two cadres "wonderous in life, glorious in death." This was also said of Liu Hulan, the subject of a "red classic" opera. See *Poyang xian zhi*, 20, 306, 939. There is also an account of this attack, with a larger death toll, in "'Jiulujun' de fumie," 117.

5. *Jiangxi sheng gongan shi*, 293.

6. The trauma created by Li Fengchun and the Ninth Route Army lingered far longer than expected. During the Cultural Revolution, Poyang citizens were still facing accusations of having aided the Ninth Route Army. Gao, *Gao Village*, 146.

7. This account is based on documents found in casefile Z1-2-590. Like the documents used for casefile 2, these reports were clearly archived by the Politics and Law Office, most likely between 1958 and the start of the Cultural Revolution in 1966. The casefile is simply listed as a "bandit" (*tufei*) case, but that was one of the few charges that were not leveled against Merchant Zha, whose full name also appears on the casefile cover. Except for the county judges, all of the names taken from the casefile in question have been changed to obscure the identities of the parties involved.

8. Z1-2-590, 26. This is a simplified version of events: he first went east to Leping County, where he briefly found another banking job, only to quickly move further east to Poyang. Ages are given here in *sui*, the traditional system for counting age in China. The Poyang bank branch was named the Raozhou Branch after an earlier name for the region. *Poyang xian zhi*, 19.

9. But the Yumin Bank built on a long history of banking in China. Banking first came to Poyang during the reign of the Tongzhi emperor, when the Qing dynasty attempted to recover from internal rebellion and imperialist invasion. In 1866 a private monetary shop opened its doors in Poyang Town,

providing credit, deposit, and remittance services. These monetary shops offered loans for survival as opposed to loans for investing. Borrowers could expect high-interest short-term loans, not too dissimilar from the rates offered by rural lenders. Poyang Town had a handful of these protomodern banking institutions, but Yumin Bank was its first fully modern enterprise when the Poyang branch opened in 1935. For an overview of Poyang banking, see *Poyang xian zhi*, 844.

10. Banking could be a fashionable job, particularly in urban centers. According to Wen-hsin Yeh: "In the early decades of the twentieth century it meant glitter and glamour to work for a Shanghai bank." Merchant Zha, of course, worked in a rural setting. Poyang Town was a far cry from Shanghai, or even Nanchang. See Wen-hsin Yeh, *Shanghai Splendor: Economic Sentiments and the Making of Modern China, 1843–1949* (Berkeley: University of California Press, 2007), 93.

11. According to a later statement, a Raozhou branch manager surnamed Kuang had connected him with a job as a secretary for the old township government office (*xiang gongsuo*) in June. At the township government office he asked three men for help; they hired him to work in the office. Zhegang Township was based at Zhegang Street (Jie) during the Republican era. The township oversaw 18 hamlets, 110 neighborhoods, and 115 natural villages. *Poyang xian zhi*, 56.

12. Military liaison: *daduifu*.

13. Quoted in Charles F. Romanus and Riley Sunderland, *China-Burma-India Theater: Time Runs Out in CBI*, vol. 1 (Washington, DC: US Government Printing Office, 1999), 369.

14. Shi Nai-an and Luo Guanzhong, 115.

15. *Poyang xian zhi*, 540–41.

16. This provision system (*bao gan zhi*) was replaced by a regular salary system in 1955 but made a comeback during the Cultural Revolution when the economy neared collapse. See Li Kwok-sing, *A Glossary of Political Terms*, 15.

17. Hengxi was the headquarters for the Sixth District in 1949 but lost that status by the end of the year. The administrative changes here complicate matters: Merchant Zha had contact with Zhegang Township, Hengxi Township, and the Sixth District headquartered in Hengxi.

18. *Jiangxi sheng gongan shi*, 6.

19. Right around this time district-chief Mo Hong'en, who assigned Merchant Zha to his post, was himself transferred. Z1–2-590, 20.

20. For old salary numbers, see *Poyang xian zhi*, 176–77.

21. Merchant Zha lived in the township's First Village, most likely right at the seat of the township government. He lived with a small but extended family of eight: himself, his wife and three children, his mother, and an aunt and uncle.

22. For an overview of commercial life in Poyang Town, see *Poyang xian zhi*, 757–59.

23. Of the 531 businesses, 71 had significant capital. This description of county market towns is from *Poyang xian zhi*, 747–59.

24. He had a second partner in his business, also from the Zhang clan.

25. For a discussion of county taxes see *Poyang xian zhi*, 822–36.

26. Each stockholder invested 1,200,000 RMB and the total investment was 4,800,000 RMB. Z1–2-590, 4

27. Bits and pieces of the story behind the opening of the press are scattered throughout the file. The most detailed account can be found in Merchant Zha's second confession. Z1–2-590, 23–24.

28. *Renmin ribao*, July 30, 1950, 3.

29. This decree was issued on October 20, 1949. According to the county government, profiteers and evildoers were purchasing farming buffaloes for slaughter and had ignored government pleas to stop. Old buffaloes that were unable to help with farming, or were truly sick, had to be brought to the tax collection office for approval for slaughter. The decree warned Poyang citizens against attempting to trick the government by making their buffaloes ill on purpose. *Poyang xian zhi*, 115. During this time oil presses were powered by human or animal labor. The county started using electricity to press oil in 1958. For more on oil production see *Poyang xian zhi*, 710.

30. "Zhonghua renmin gongheguo tudi gaige fa" (June 28, 1950), in *Zhongguo tudi gaige shiliao xuanbian* [Selected historical materials from China's land reform] (Beijing: Guofang Daxue Chubanshe, 1988), 642–47.

31. By this point the Sixth District government offices, originally headquartered in Hengxi, should have been moved fourteen miles away to Langbu Village. See *Poyang xian zhi*, 57.

32. The relationship between district governments and branches of the People's Tribunal is of course unexplained in the documents. It seems, however, that there was significant overlap between the two. Also unexplained in the casefile is why Merchant Zha chose to bring his case to this particular tribunal. There was a closer tribunal in Youdunjie. See *Poyang xian zhi*, 445. But given the importance of water transport in Poyang, Forty Mile Street may have been an easier trip.

33. Ibid., 4.

34. Merchant Zha's rhetoric was very much in line with the words now favored by the Communists. But his explanation of his woes also deviated from party rhetoric when he blamed the "extreme ignorance of the villagers" (*laobiao wuzhi de hen duo*). Z1–2-590, 6.

35. Ibid., 7.

36. Ibid., 8–9.

37. Ibid., 20.

38. Ibid., 21–22.

39. Ibid., 24.

40. Ibid., 24–25.

41. The opinion of the masses for this case is listed as only requesting a conviction. The official ruling, making reference to the ongoing national

campaign to suppress counterrevolutionaries, was approved by the Fuliang Prefectural Party Committee. Z1-2-590, 34–35.

42. It is unclear if Judge Wang was ruling from a branch tribunal, or the county tribunal. Z1–2-590, 33.

43. Ibid., 26–27.

44. Ibid., 27–28.

45. In reflection of this change, the characters for "counterrevolutionary" (*fandong fenzi*) are crossed out on one of the case's cover pages. Z1-2-590, 32.

46. Ibid., 37.

47. Gao, *Gao Village*, 94–95.

A Few More Words in Closing

1. In 1944 two clans squared off in violent conflict to determine who would control their corner of rural China. The Zhang family lost, but they refused to submit. Zhang Guohua had served in the Nationalist army, while his clansman Zhang Liangyuan had served as a township head. Five years before the Communists declared the start of New China, the two men took to the mountains as bandits. As outlaws had done for thousands of years they roamed the borders between counties to better evade state power. Relying on high mountains and deep forests, they established almost two dozen strategically placed strongholds. The Nationalists never had the time or interest to root the Zhang men out of the mountains. There were, after all, Communists to exterminate. But regimes change. After the Communists came to power they were determined to get rid of the Zhang bandits, whose old ties to the Nationalist order made them particularly troublesome. Multiple attempts to rid the mountains of the Zhang outlaws, however, uniformly failed. All the while, the Jiangxi countryside endured years of changes. Land reform gave land to peasants. Then a long process of collectivization took the land right back and gave it to the state. In 1957 the Zhangs were still holding out in the Jiangxi hinterlands. That year the Communists sent over 2,000 men to assault their latest mountain lair, only to learn that their targets had donned disguises and escaped right under their noses. A few months later, Jiangxi security officers finally discovered a weakness that they could exploit: the two bandits, perhaps for reasons that cannot be mentioned in local histories, were quietly visiting a widow at night. During the day they helped her cut firewood and plant crops, secretly delivering the goods to her at night. What they obtained in return, who can ever know? On the night of June 29, 1958, security officers made their move. Coordinating with a local militia, they surrounded the widow's house and attacked, shooting and killing Zhang Liangyuan. Zhang Guohua escaped and returned to the mountains, far from the widow that had nearly cost him his life. Two years later, in late 1960, he finally met his end, accidentally and unceremoniously killed in a makeshift boar trap. *Jiangxi sheng gongan shi: 1949–1959*, 290, 297–99.

BIBLIOGRAPHY

Poyang County Public Security Bureau Casefiles
"Materials on Poyang County, Northern Poyang Spies, Bandits, and Secret Society Activity" (Poyang xian Pobei tewu tufei huimen huodong cailiao). Casefile Z2–1-52.
"Li XX (Big Tiger)" (Li XX (Da laohu). Casefile Z1-3–329.
"Materials on a Fake 'Peasant Association'" (Jia "nonghui" cailiao). Casefile Z2–3-21.
"Bandit Zha XX" (Tufei Zha XX). Casefile Z1–2-590.

Published Sources
"Abstract of Peking Gazettes." *North-China Herald and Supreme Court and Consular Gazette*, January 14, 1875, 27.
Averill, Stephen C. "Party, Society, and Local Elite in the Jiangxi Communist Movement." *Journal of Asian Studies* 46, no. 2 (May 1987): 279–303.
"Bandits Feared at Poyang. Sporadic Attacks by Communist Marauders." *North-China Herald and Supreme Court and Consular Gazette*, March 1, 1933, 332.
Billingsley, Philip. *Bandits in Republican China*. Stanford, CA: Stanford University Press, 1988.
Bo Yibo. *Ruogan zhongda juece yu shijian de huigu* [Recollections on some major policy decisions and events]. Beijing: Zhonggong zhongyang dang xiao chubanshi, 1991.
Brown, Jeremy. "From Resisting Communists to Resisting America: Civil War and Korean War in Southwest China, 1950–1951." In *Dilemmas of Victory: The Early Years of the People's Republic of China*, edited by Jeremy Brown and Paul. G. Pickowicz, 105–29. Cambridge, MA: Harvard University Press, 2007.
Brown, Jeremy, and Matthew David Johnson. "Introduction." In *Maoism at the Grassroots*, edited by Jeremy Brown and Matthew David Johnson, 1–18. Cambridge, MA: Harvard University Press, 2015.

Chang Kuo-sin. *Eight Months Behind the Bamboo Curtain: A Report on the First Eight Months of Communist Rule in China.* Hong Kong: City University Hong Kong Press, 2016.

Chen Ming. *Wo yu Ding Ling wushi nian* [My fifty years with Ding Ling]. Beijing: Zhongguo da baike quanshu chubanshe, 2010.

Cunningham, R. "When the Bamboo Flowers." *North-China Herald and Supreme Court and Consular Gazette*, September 30, 1916, 691.

Davis, Edward L. *Society and the Supernatural in Song China.* Honolulu: University of Hawai'i Press, 2001.

DeMare, Brian James. *Land Wars: The Story of China's Agrarian Revolution.* Stanford, CA: Stanford University Press, 2019.

DeMare, Brian James. *Mao's Cultural Army: Drama Troupes in China's Rural Revolution.* Cambridge: Cambridge University Press, 2015.

Deng Zihui, "Cong Eqian xiang douzheng lai yanjiu muqian tudigaige yundong" [From Eqian Township struggle to researching current land reform movement]. In *Zhongguo tudi gaige shiliao xuanbian* [Selected historical materials from China's land reform]. Beijing: Guofang daxue chubanshe, 1988.

Diamant, Neil J. *Revolutionizing the Family: Politics, Love, and Divorce in Urban and Rural China, 1949–1968.* Berkeley: University of California Press, 2000.

DuBois, Thomas David. *The Sacred Village: Social Change and Religious Life in Rural North China.* Honolulu: University of Hawai'i Press, 2005.

Duchang xian zhi [Duchang County gazetteer]. Beijing: Xinhua chubanshe, 1992.

Eisenman, Joshua. *Red China's Green Revolution: Technological Innovation, Institutional Change, and Economic Development Under the Commune.* New York: Columbia University Press, 2018.

Esherick, Joseph W. "Ten Theses on the Chinese Revolution." *Modern China* 21, no. 1 (January 1995): 45–76.

Esherick, Joseph W. *The Origins of the Boxer Uprising.* Berkeley: University of California Press, 1987.

Friedman, Edward, Paul G. Pickowicz, and Mark Selden. *Chinese Village, Socialist State.* New Haven, CT: Yale University Press, 1993.

Friedman, Edward, Paul G. Pickowicz, and Mark Selden. *Revolution, Resistance, and Reform in Village China.* New Haven, CT: Yale University Press, 2005.

Gao, James *The Communist Takeover of Hangzhou: The Transformation of City and Cadre, 1949–1954.* Honolulu: University of Hawai'i Press, 2004.

Gao, Mobo C. F. *Gao Village: Modern Life in Rural China.* Honolulu: University of Hawai'i Press, 1995.

Gao, Mobo C. F. *Gao Village Revisited: The Life of Rural People in Contemporary China.* New York: Columbia University Press, 2019.

Goldman, Merlie. "The Party and the Intellectuals." In *The Cambridge History of China*, edited by Roderick MacFarquhar and John K. Fairbank, 218–58. Cambridge: Cambridge University Press, 1987.

Hershatter, Gail. *The Gender of Memory: Rural Women and China's Collective Past*. Berkeley: University of California Press, 2011.

Hou, Xiaojia. *Negotiating Socialism in Rural China: Mao, Peasants, and Local Cadres in Shanxi, 1949–1953*. Ithaca, NY: Cornell East Asia Series, 2016.

Huang, Philip. *Chinese Civil Justice, Past and Present*. Lanham, MD: Rowman and Littlefield, 2010.

Huang, Philip. *The Peasant Economy and Social Change in North China*. Stanford, CA: Stanford University Press, 1988.

Huang, Philip. *The Peasant Family and Rural Development in the Yangzi Delta, 1350–1988*. Stanford, CA: Stanford University Press, 1990.

"Imperial Decrees." *North-China Herald and Supreme Court and Consular Gazette*, June 19, 1901, 1188.

"In the Yangtse Valley. III—Hankow and the British Surrender." *Irish Times*, May 3, 1927, 11.

"Japan Bombs Imperil Americans. United States Warships Race to Swatow, South China Port, to Evacuate Nationals; 500 Killed and Wounded Toll of Air Raids." *Los Angeles Times*, July 3, 1938, 1.

"Japanese Extend Range of Bombing. Many Cities, Railways, Aerodromes Attacked and Number of Chinese Planes Destroyed." *North-China Herald and Supreme Court and Consular Gazette*, December 22, 1937, 445.

Javed, Jeffery A. *Righteous Revolutionaries: Morality, Mobilization, and Violence in the Making of the Chinese State*. Ann Arbor: University of Michigan Press, 2022.

Jiangxi sheng fayuan zhi [Jiangxi Province court gazetteer]. Fangzhi chuban she, 1996.

Jiangxi sheng gongan shi: 1949–1959 [Jiangxi province public security history, 1949–1959]. Nanchang: Jiangxi sheng gongan ting, 1994.

Jiangxi sheng sifa xingzheng zhi [Jiangxi province judicial administration gazetteer]. Jiangxi renmin chubanshe, 1995.

Kiely, Jan. *The Compelling Ideal: Thought Reform and the Prison in China, 1901–1956*. New Haven, CT: Yale University Press, 2014.

Kuhn, Philip. *Soulstealers: The Chinese Sorcery Scare of 1768*. Cambridge, MA: Harvard University Press, 1992.

"Lake Is Reddened by Chinese Battle. Japanese Gain West Bank of Poyang in Week-Long Fight." *Atlanta Constitution*, July 25, 1938, 16.

Leese, Daniel, and Puck Engman, editors. *Victims, Perpetrators, and the Role of Law in Maoist China: A Case-Study Approach*. Berlin: De Gruyter, 2020.

Li, Kwok-sing, *A Glossary of Political Terms of the People's Republic of China*. Translated by Mary Lok. Hong Kong: The Chinese University of Hong Kong Press, 1995.

Li, Huaiyin. *Village Governance in North China: 1875–1936*. Stanford, CA: Stanford University Press, 2005.

"'Jiulujun' de fumie" [The destruction of the "Ninth Route Army"]. In *Qing jiao fei te de gushi* [Stories of eliminating bandits and spies], edited by Li Qingshan, 133–46. Beijing: Zhonggong dangshi chubanshe, 2004.

Liu Shigu, "'Shixu' xia de 'zhixu': xin Zhongguo chengli chuqi tugai zhong de sifa Shijian—dui Poyang xian 'bufa dizhu an' de jiedu yu fenxi" ["Order" under "disorder": Judicial practice during New China establishment initial period land reform—An interpretation and analysis of "illegal landlord cases" in Poyang County]. *Jinshidai yanjiu* [Contemporary history research], no. 6 (2015): 91—105.

Liu, Shigu, "Using Local Public Security Archives from the 1950s—Poyang County, Jiangxi." In *Fieldwork in Modern Chinese History: A Research Guide*, edited by Thomas David DuBois and Jan Keily, 282–88. New York: Routledge, 2020.

McDermott, Joseph P. "Book Collecting in Jiangxi." In *Knowledge and Text Production in an Age of Print—China, 900–1400*, edited by Lucille Chia and Hilde De Weerdt, 63–101. Leiden: Brill, 2011.

Mühlhahn, Klaus. *Criminal Justice in China: A History*. Cambridge MA: Harvard University Press, 2009.

"Notes from the Native Papers: Shenpao." *North-China Herald and Supreme Court and Consular Gazette*, July 15, 1892, 98

Neibu cankao [Internal reference materials]. Beijing: Xinhua chubanshe.

Noellert, Matthew. *Power over Property: The Political Economy of Communist Land Reform in China*. Ann Arbor: University of Michigan Press, 2020.

"Notes from Kiangsi." *North-China Herald and Supreme Court and Consular Gazette*, February 3, 1917, 220.

"100,000 Move on Chinese Bandits. Nanking Authorities Also Use Planes in Attack on Communists." *Louisville Courier-Journal*, November 3, 1930, 1.

Perry, Elizabeth J. "Making Communism Work: Sinicizing a Soviet Governance Practice." *Comparative Studies in Society and History* 61, no. 3 (2019): 535–62.

Perry, Elizabeth J. "The Promise of PRC History." *Journal of Modern Chinese History* 10, no. 1 (January 2016): 113–17.

Perry, Elizabeth J. *Rebels and Revolutionaries in North China, 1845–1945*. Stanford, CA: Stanford University Press, 1980.

Poyang xian zhi [Poyang County gazetteer]. Beijing: Fangzhi chubanshe, 2010.

Reed, Bradley. *Talons and Teeth: County Clerks and Runners in the Qing Dynasty*. Stanford, CA: Stanford University Press, 2000.

Renmin ribao [The people's daily]. Beijing: Renmin ribao she.

"Rising Yangtze Threatens Greatest Flood Since '31." *New York Times*, July 11, 1949, 8.

Rittenberg, Sidney. *The Man Who Stayed Behind*. Durham, NC: Duke University Press, 2001.

Romanus, Charles F., and Riley Sunderland, *China-Burma-India Theater: Time Runs Out in CBI*. Vol. 1. Washington, DC: US. Government Printing Office, 1999.

Rowe, William. *China's Last Empire: The Great Qing*. Cambridge, MA: Belknap Press, 2012.

Schoenhals, Michael. *Spying for the People: Mao's Secret Agents, 1949–1967*. Cambridge: Cambridge University Press, 2013.

Shepard, Wade. *Ghost Cities of China: The Story of Cities without People in the World's Most Populated Country*. London: Zed Books, 2015.

Shi Nai-an, and Luo Guanzhong. *Outlaws of the Marsh*. Translated by Sidney Shapiro. Bloomington: Indiana University Press, 1981.

Sixiang wenti [Ideological problems]. Beijing: Sanlian shudian, 1950.

Smith, Aminda M. *Thought Reform and China's Dangerous Classes: Reeducation, Resistance, and the People*. Lanham, MD: Rowman and Littlefield, 2012.

"Soldiers Set Out to Save Captured Hanyang Priest. 2,500 Troops Seek Trace of Rev. Lalor in Wuhan Area." *China Press*, May 24, 1928, 18.

Strauss, Julia. "Paternalist Terror: The Campaign to Suppress Counterrevolutionaries and Regime Consolidation in the People's Republic of China, 1950–1953." *Society for Comparative Study of Society and History* 44, no. 1 (2002): 80–105.

Strauss, Julia. *State Formation in China and Taiwan: Bureaucracy, Campaign, and Performance*. Cambridge: Cambridge University Press, 2019.

Thaxton, Ralph. *Catastrophe and Contention in Rural China: Mao's Great Leap Forward Famine and the Origins of Righteous Resistance in Da Fo Village*. Cambridge: Cambridge University Press, 2008.

Von Glahn, Richard. *The Sinister Way: The Divine and the Demonic in Chinese Religious Culture*. Berkeley: University of California Press, 2004.

Wang, Di. *The Teahouse under Socialism: The Decline and Renewal of Public Life in Chengdu, 1959–2000*. Ithaca, NY: Cornell University Press, 2018.

Wang, Di. *Violence and Order on the Chengdu Plain: The Story of a Secret Brotherhood in Rural China, 1939–1949*. Stanford, CA: Stanford University Press, 2018.

Wemheuer, Felix. *A Social History of Maoist China: Conflict and Change, 1949–1976*. Cambridge: Cambridge University Press, 2019.

Westad, Odd Arne. *Decisive Encounters: The Chinese Civil War*. Stanford, CA: Stanford University Press, 2003.

Williams, Philip F., and Yenna Wu. *The Great Wall of Confinement: The*

Chinese Prison Camp through Contemporary Fiction and Reportage.
Berkeley: University of California Press, 2004.

Xi Zhongxun, "Guanyu tugai zhong yixie wenti gei Mao zhuxi de baogao"
[A report to Chairman Mao concerning some problems in land reform].
In *Zhongguo tudi gaige shiliao xuanbian* [Selected historical materials
from China's land reform]. Beijing: Guofang daxue chubanshe, 1988.

Yang Kuisong. *Eight Outcasts: Social and Political Marginalization in China
under Mao.* Translated by Gregor Benton and Ye Zhan. Oakland: University of California Press, 2019.

Xu Hongci. *No Wall Too High: One Man's Daring Escape from Mao's
Darkest Prison.* Translated and edited by Erling Hoh. New York: Sarah
Crichton Books, 2017.

Yeh, Wen-hsin. *Shanghai Splendor: Economic Sentiments and the Making
of Modern China, 1843–1949.* Berkeley: University of California Press,
2007.

"Zhonghua renmin gongheguo tudi gaige fa" [Land reform law of the
People's Republic of China]. In *Zhongguo tudi gaige shiliao xuanbian*
[Selected historical materials from China's land reform]. Beijing: Guofang
daxue chubanshe, 1988.

INDEX

Page numbers in italics denote illustration

Lightning Source UK Ltd.
Milton Keynes UK
UKHW010155070722
405476UK00003B/124

9 781503 632363